v Children
with Down Syndrome Learn

renamed Stars of Success

Proven and Effective Instructional Techniques for Parents and Professionals

Susan J. Peoples

Special Offspring Publishing, L.L.C.
Fort Wayne, Indiana

Portions of the text are copywritten by the National Down Syndrome Society and
reprinted here with permission. The mission of NDSS is to benefit people with
Down syndrome and their families through national leadership in education,
research and advocacy. For more information call (800) 221-4602 or visit
www.ndss.org.

ISBN: 0-9752639-0-0

Special Offspring Publishing, L.L.C.
5010 Lodge Pole Lane
Fort Wayne, IN 46814
(260) 625-6493
www.specialoffspring.com
or
www.specialoffspring.com
e-mail: specialoffspring@aol.com

Printed in the United States of America

Preface[3]

Dear Teacher,

I am a survivor of a concentration camp.
My eyes saw what no man should witness.

Gas chambers built by *learned* engineers.
Children poisoned by *educated* physicians.
Infants killed by *trained* nurses.
Women & babies shot & burned by *high school &
    college* graduates.

So I am suspicious of education.
My request is: Help your students
    become human.
Your efforts must never
    produce learned monsters, skilled
    psychopaths, educated Eichmanns.
Reading, writing, arithmetic are
    important only if they serve to make our
    children more humane.

How we educate our children today will determine tomorrow's future.

[3]Ginott, Haim G. <u>Teacher and Child</u>. New York: Collier, 1995.

Acknowledgements

On the surface writing appears to be a solitary occupation. In fact, it takes numerous people to produce a book. I am grateful to quite a few. I am indebted to all the people who helped me in this process.

Firstly, special thanks to Vernell Fettiq, whose razor-sharp editing perfected this manuscript. I am a better person as well as writer because of Vernell's talents and friendship.

I would like to express my deepest gratitude to Joe Bockerstette, whose belief in the need to distribute this material is the sole reason this book was written. Joe's unending patience, time, encouragement, exceptional editorial skills, and love for his family, especially beautiful little Amy who has Down syndrome, have resulted in a simple reference manual that we hope will touch the lives of children with Down syndrome in a positive way forever!

I must also express sincere appreciation to Libby Kumin and Patricia Oelwein, both of whom are dedicated to enhancing the lives of children with Down syndrome. Had it not been for the work of these two fine ladies, little would be available to guide and assist teachers and parents of children with Down syndrome. You both have made a difference in the world in which we live!

Additionally, I must recognize Mrs. Kitty Wehrli, deceased, founder of the Wehrli Learning Fitness Program. Words cannot describe the depth of respect and appreciation I feel for Kitty Wehrli and her work. The only master teacher that I have had the privilege to know, Kitty spent four years as my mentor, helping me to save my son Michael from his path of self-destruction, born of academic frustration, and transform him back into the beautiful gift of a little boy I once had. It was

Kitty's knowledge and development of the Wehrli Learning Fitness Program that empowered Michael to systematically tackle academic challenges and progress positively in the school environment.

I must also thank Mrs. Nancy Buck and Mrs. Judy Stamwitz for giving so generously of time they really did not have to review, constructively criticize, and offer opinions on the final manuscript. I appreciate and respect their talents.

Most of all, I would like to express my most heartfelt appreciation to the wonderful family that I have been blessed with the privilege of calling mine: my husband Steve, my daughters Katie and Betsy, and my sons Thomas and Michael. Thank you so much for your support and unending love for Michael who has Down syndrome. You are my inspirations, my everything.

Lastly, I embrace my mother, Betty James, with complete love and respect. She has taught me well how to love family and catch my dreams. In her words, "You can do anything you want, as long as you are willing to work hard enough to achieve it." My desire is to take some of the hardships away for children with Down syndrome.

Thank you all!

Susan J. Peoples
March 2003

Introduction

Stars of Success is a book of insights. The methods and instructional techniques discussed are the result of 27 years as an elementary school teacher, eleven years as the mother of a beautiful boy named Michael, hundreds of hours of clinical observation of children with Down syndrome in educational and social settings, and a compilation of lifelong studies by experts in the fields related to educating children with Down syndrome and other developmental delays.

The body of the text summarizes the1996 educational inclusion study from the National Down Syndrome Society. The "Author's Additional Comments" and "Author's Instructional Suggestions" expand the findings of renowned authors by extrapolating from them successful techniques for practical classroom and home applications.

While searching for the means by which to help my son learn, I was inspired to share my knowledge by two incidents that occured in recent years. The following stories underscore my reasons for writing this book.

While chatting with other parents, I discovered that many children with Down syndrome were receiving financial support from their insurance carriers for speech therapy. What a relief! At the time, I was driving one hour each way for speech therapy at a cost of one hundred dollars an hour! Because my husband was employed by a large company, our family had medical coverage by a universally known insurance company. I wrote them immediately.

Within a month, I received a reply. It had been determined that Michael had Down syndrome and, therefore, was "uneducable." I could not have been more enraged! The word "uneducable" was from the Dark Ages! Well, I provided that company with an avalanche of documentation proving that children with Down syndrome can and do learn. I contacted universities, medical centers, authors of books on children with Down syndrome, pediatricians, and schools. Nine months later, Michael received insurance support as I hope many other children with Down syndrome did from that point forward.

Not long after the insurance incident, while riding in the car one day, my then twelve-year-old daughter, Betsy asked, "Mom, if you could take Michael's Down syndrome away, would you do it?" Without hesitation I replied, "No, I would take away all his hardships, but I'd never take the Down syndrome away." She said, "I knew you would say that Mom."

My intent for this book is to take away some of the hardships. If only one child is touched but one time by only one suggestion from these tips, then all of my time and effort will have been worthwhile.

Table of Contents

Down Syndrome: Myths & Truths[5]

All children with Down syndrome are individuals first. While progress has been made in educating children with Down syndrome, there is still enormous opportunity for further progress. This text is intended to provide insight into the mental processing of children with Down syndrome and provide better educational programs. The material found in this book will hold true for most children with Down syndrome and some or all of the learning characteristics discussed may be inherent to any student with Down syndrome. However, I do not imply that the methods presented here will hold true for every child with Down syndrome.

Additionally, all children with Down syndrome are developmentally delayed. Unique genetic, physical, and health problems make children with Down syndrome easily recognizable; however, children with Down syndrome are only a segment of the greater population of children with developmental delays. For this reason, the "Author's Additional Comments" and "Author's Instructional Suggestions" will also apply to many children in the greater community of children with developmental delays.

MYTH: *Down syndrome is a rare genetic disorder.*

TRUTH: Down syndrome is the most commonly occurring genetic condition. One in every 800 to 1,000 live births is a child with Down syndrome, representing approximately 5,000 births per year in the United States alone. Today, Down syndrome affects more than 350,000 people in the United States.

MYTH: *Most children with Down syndrome are born to older parents.*

---

[5]Adapted from National Down Syndrome Society. Down Syndrome: Facts and Resources. New York: NDSS.

TRUTH: Eighty percent of children born with Down syndrome are born to women younger than 35 years old. As a woman ages, however, her chance of conceiving a child with Down syndrome becomes greater.

MYTH: *People with Down syndrome are severely retarded.*

TRUTH: Most people with Down syndrome have IQ's that fall in the mild to moderate range of retardation. Children with Down syndrome are definitely educable. Educators and researchers are still discovering the full educational potential of people with Down syndrome.

MYTH: *Most people with Down syndrome are institutionalized.*

TRUTH: Today people with Down syndrome live at home with their families and are active participants in the educational, vocational, social, and recreational activities of the community. They are integrated into the regular educational system and engage in sports, camping, music and art programs, and other community activities. In addition, they socialize with people with and without disabilities, and as adults, are obtaining employment and living in group homes or other independent housing arrangements.

MYTH: *Parents will not find community support in bringing up their child with Down syndrome.*

TRUTH: In almost every community of the United States, parent support groups and other community organizations are directly involved in providing services to families of individuals with Down syndrome.

MYTH: *Children with Down syndrome must be placed in segregated special education programs.*

TRUTH: Children with Down syndrome have been included in regular academic classrooms in schools across the country. In some instances, they are integrated into specific courses while, in other situations, students are fully included in the regular classroom for all subjects. The degree of mainstreaming is based on the abilities of the individual; today the trend is for full inclusion in the social and educational life of the community.

MYTH: *Adults with Down syndrome are unemployable.*

TRUTH: Businesses are seeking young adults with Down syndrome for a variety of positions. Adults with Down syndrome are being employed in offices, by banks, corporations, nursing homes, hotels and restaurants. Down syndrome adults work in the music and entertainment industry, clerical positions, and the computer industry. People with Down syndrome typically bring to their jobs enthusiasm, reliability, and dedication.

MYTH: *People with Down syndrome are always happy.*

TRUTH: People with Down syndrome have a wide range of feelings just like everyone else. All persons with Down syndrome respond to positive expressions of friendship and are hurt and upset by inconsiderate behavior.

MYTH: *Adults with Down syndrome cannot form relationships leading to marriage.*

TRUTH: People with Down syndrome date, socialize, and form on-going relationships. Some marry. Women with Down syndrome can and do have children; and there is a 50 percent chance that their child will have Down syndrome. Although rare, men with Down syndrome can father children.

MYTH: *Down syndrome is untreatable.*

TRUTH: Through early intervention, speech therapy, physical therapy, and occupational therapy, it is possible to improve many of the problems associated with Down syndrome. In addition, research on Down syndrome is making significant

3

strides in identifying the genes on chromosome 21 that cause the characteristics of Down syndrome. Scientists now feel strongly that it will be possible to improve, correct, or prevent many of the problems associated with Down syndrome in the future.

MYTH: *Children with Down syndrome "plateau."*

TRUTH: Learning is a lifelong experience for people with Down syndrome, just like everyone else. The idea that a child with Down syndrome would "plateau" or decline in rate of development is more likely due to an educational program that does not continue to meet the individual needs of the student.

What Is Down Syndrome?[5]

Down syndrome is a genetic condition that affects people of all ages, races, and economic levels and is the most frequently occurring chromosomal abnormality.

The most common form of Down syndrome, Trisomy 21, occurs when three (instead of two) number 21 chromosomes exist in every cell of the body. Instead of the usual 46 chromosomes, a person with Trisomy 21 has 47. This additional genetic material alters the course of development and causes the characteristics associated with Down syndrome.

Although it is well established that the incidence of Down syndrome increases with the age of the mother, the cause of the extra chromosome that leads to Down syndrome is still unknown. No connection has been found between the parents' activities before or during pregnancy and the occurrence of Down syndrome.

Down syndrome is usually identified at birth by the presence of certain physical traits: low muscle tone, a single deep crease across the palm of the hand, a slightly flattened facial profile, and an upward slant to the eyes. Because these features may be present in babies without Down syndrome, a chromosomal analysis must be done to confirm the diagnosis.

All people with Down syndrome have some level of mental retardation. That level usually falls into the mild to moderate range, however, and is not indicative of the many strengths and talents each individual possesses.

Individuals with Down syndrome are becoming increasingly included in society and community organizations such as school, health care systems, work forces, and social and recreational activities. Due to advances in medical technology,

[5]Adapted from National Down Syndrome Society. Down Syndrome: Facts and Resources. New York: NDSS.

individuals with Down syndrome are living longer than ever before. In 1910, children with Down syndrome were expected to survive to age 9. With the discovery of antibiotics, the average survival age increased to 19 to 20. With recent advancements in clinical treatment, as many as 80 percent of adults with Down syndrome now reach age 55, and many live even longer. In the United States, approximately 350,000 people are affected by Down syndrome. Approximately 5,000 children with Down syndrome are born each year. As the mortality rate associated with Down syndrome is decreasing, the prevalence of individuals with Down syndrome in our society will increase. More and more Americans will interact with individuals with this genetic condition, increasing the need for widespread public education and acceptance.

Down syndrome is a developmental disability. As researchers learn more about the molecular genetics and other aspects of Down syndrome, they also obtain valuable information about human development and can advance the study of many biological processes. In addition, individuals with Down syndrome have a higher incidence of certain medical problems, and the study of Down syndrome may yield important breakthroughs in those areas. Research in Down syndrome provides a way of looking at many other prevalent medical conditions:

Heart defects – Up to 50 percent of individuals with Down syndrome are born with congenital heart defects. The majority of heart defects in children with Down syndrome can now be surgically corrected with resulting long–term health improvements. Scientists continue to search for the cause and prevention of this problem.

Alzheimer's disease – Estimates vary, but it is reasonable to conclude that 25 percent or more of individuals with Down syndrome over the age of 35 will develop the clinical signs and symptoms of Alzheimer's-type dementia.

Leukemia – Individuals with Down syndrome have a 15 to 20

times greater risk of developing leukemia. The majority of cases are categorized as acute megakaryoblastic leukemia, which tends to occur in the first three years of life, and for which there is a high cure rate. In newborns with Down syndrome, a transient form of leukemia is also seen, but disappears spontaneously during the first two to three months of life.

AUTHOR'S ADDITIONAL COMMENTS

To provide children the most comprehensive and successful school experience, practitioners should be aware of physical characteristics and health conditions that affect student success.

The key is success. To comprehend how important the premise of success is, the frustration of the developmentally delayed child must be understood. From birth, children with Down syndrome frequently endure failure due to delays in developmental milestones, such as walking and talking. In the morning, most children jump out of bed, rush to the bathroom, brush their teeth, put on their clothes, and race downstairs. The child experiencing physical challenges and developmental delays, however, gets out of bed, goes to the bathroom and is confronted with the toothpaste cap. The struggles begin. The simple activity of dressing and undressing poses even greater challenges. By the time developmentally challenged children make it downstairs in the morning, they have already overcome innumerable obstacles and frustrations. Therefore, the school experience must provide a safe environment, rich in successful experiences!

There are several common physical features among children with Down syndrome that may directly affect student performance:

- Muscle hypotonia – low muscle tone,
- Increased tactile sensitivity,
- Enlargement of tongue in relationship to size of mouth,
- Compact skeletal structure of facial features.

7

Muscle hypotonia – To understand the physical demands of reduced muscle tone, imagine completing tasks of daily living with a pair of socks on your hands.

1) Frustration results when the student knows how to do something, but the skill required to complete the task (i.e. circling or underlining) is difficult for him. Analyze all responses. Perceived "bad" behavior may actually be a result of processing, language, and/or tactile differences.

2) Allow extra time and provide increased opportunities for skills practice. Remember that simple requests to hang up a coat, use the bathroom, or complete written assignments are major challenges.

3) Muscle development requires consistent and repetitive training. It is important that specific muscle development needs be identified and improved.

4) Avoidance behaviors need to be carefully analyzed. The phrase "I'm tired" may be accurate because muscle hypotonia significantly increases physical demands. This phrase should be acknowledged with "I understand, let's try anyhow." That same phrase may also mean a writing task has created tired fingers. Opening and closing finger exercises may be beneficial to the student to help complete the activity. "I'm tired" may also relate to task difficulty.[12]

Increased tactile sensitivity – Individuals with Down syndrome may be more sensitive to, and upset by, tactile experiences.

1) Expose children with Down syndrome to many different fabrics, arts and craft materials, and foods to reduce resistance to tactile differences.

2) Separate tactile sensitivity behaviors (i.e., refusal to participate in art activities that require touching substances such as clay, glue, finger paint) from behavioral problems. Anxiety created by upsetting tactile experiences can result in physiological

8

complaints such as stomach pain, or a headache.

3) Give special attention to the student's writing or coloring preference. No. 2 pencils, markers, colored pencils, pens and crayons all generate different physical sensations.[12]

4) Consider tactile sensitivity related to writing instrument's grip, size, and length.

Enlargement of tongue in relationship to size of mouth – Intelligibility of speech is a problem for many children with Down syndrome. Recall the experience and intelligibility of your own speech when attempting to talk with your mouth full. Factors affecting intelligibility are low muscle tone in the mouth area, jaw movement difficulties, motor planning difficulties for speech (stuttering), rate, and fluency.[3,4,8]

1) Carefully evaluate the speech patterns of the student. Speech therapy and an oral motor exercise program can help children with Down syndrome to communicate intelligibly.[8]

2) Frequently a significant difference is measured between the receptive language ability (language understanding) and the expressive language ability (language production). Generally, receptive language ability is measured much higher than the expressive ability. This difference may be due in part to the means of evaluation. Language comprehension can be evaluated by the demonstration of understanding through pointing or following directions. Speaking, however, which presents many difficulties for children with Down syndrome, is the sole measure of expressive language. Speech may be marked by articulation errors. These lower the child's speech intelligibility and makes the child appear seemingly unintelligent. Assist the child in closing the gap between receptive language and expressive language ability. The child's "peer group acceptance" may hinge on the ability to close this gap.[4]

3) Provide one-on-one instruction for articulation skills. The

language development plan, although designed and supervised by the speech/language pathologist, should be an ongoing component of the broader IEP.

4) When stuttering or hesitation exists on initial sound production, consider faster pacing (speed with which verbalization is generated) in speech production. Ask the child to "talk fast." Although this may seem counterintuitive, faster pacing eliminates the focus on mental obstacles interfering with speech production. Practicing "robotic talk" or asking the student to "slow down" may actually increase the intensity of effort on a mental roadblock and may intensify the hesitation or stuttering.[12]

5) Recognize that an increase or decrease in stuttering can be a barometer of a child's stress level. Stuttering may significantly intensify as environmental and internal stress increases and usually diminishes as the child's comfort level increases.

6) Organize and utilize a communication team. Speech remediation will not occur in isolation within a speech therapy room. The speech/language pathologist is only part of the team. Other members may include

- Occupational therapist – works on developing postural control required for speech.

- School psychologist – measures the child's cognitive level. The degree of cognitive impairment will directly impact speech/language learning.

- Audiologist – measures child's hearing ability. Many children with Down syndrome have some degree of hearing loss.

It is the communication team that has the expertise to develop and assist the child to learn the skills needed for speech/language. It is essential that the team communicate regularly in order to share oral motor exercises and sound production techniques.[4]

Compact structure of ear, nose, and throat – The compact bone and soft tissue structure of the ear, nose and throat anatomy (i.e., sinuses, pharynx, or eustachian tubes) of the child with Down syndrome may increase susceptibility to, and severity of, sinus and upper respiratory infections and increase sensitivity to loud sounds and/or vibrations.

1) Learn about noise/vibration sensitivities and be aware of activity noise levels. The child with Down syndrome may cover his ears, run from, or avoid activities creating loud sounds or intense vibrations, i.e., fire drills, buzzing light fixtures, or band concerts. These noises can be a very real phenomenon to children with Down syndrome.

2) Pay special attention to weather conditions creating intense thunder or wind. Children with Down syndrome may respond with panic due to a heightened sensitivity to sounds.

3) Parents need to be aware that hair clippers may elicit extreme physical reactions during a haircut. Your child is not being bad. An increased sensitivity to vibrations from hair clippers may be responsible for unexpected behavior. Consider using scissors.

Other health concerns common to individuals with Down syndrome

As discussed earlier, an increased risk for certain health problems exists in individuals with Down syndrome. In addition to those previously discussed, frequently occurring conditions that may directly affect the school experience are
· Sleep apnea,
· Hearing, vision and thyroid problems.

Undiagnosed and untreated, these conditions may further

interfere with development, learning, and behavior. The best teaching and behavior management programs are ineffective in addressing academic challenges if the cause is misunderstood or overlooked.[5,9,4,8,11]

Sleep Apnea – The cessation of airflow in the nose and mouth (breathing) for more than 15 seconds may be a "double-edge" condition. Sleep apnea can make a child either more tired or, conversely, more hyperactive.[11]

1) Investigate continued lethargic behaviors. Complications of sleep apnea such as memory loss and intellectual impairment may intensify the academic and social challenges already facing a child with Down syndrome and may inaccurately be interpreted as an attention deficit disorder.

2) Recognize that fatigue resulting from sleep apnea may also manifest itself as hyperactive behavior in some children. Recent studies at the University of Michigan suggest a link between sleep disorders and ADHD. "If kids express daytime sleepiness differently than adults, their hyperactivity could be a way of staying awake."[1]

3) Explore sleep patterns, such as snoring, with parents. Simple medical interventions may be available that could transform an otherwise inattentive or hyperactive child (ADHD) into a better student.

Hearing, vision and thyroid problems – Because of the anatomical differences in the ear structure (narrow and short canals), children with Down syndrome are more susceptible to hearing problems. Approximately 65 to 80 percent have some conductive hearing loss and about 50 percent of all people with Down syndrome have vision problems. There is also a higher incidence of hypothyroidism (an under-active thyroid gland). Hypothyroidism can cause sluggishness, skin dryness, and weight gain and also may further impair the child mentally.[3,4,8,11]

1) Request an annual hearing and vision screening by a

physician qualified to evaluate children with special needs.

2) Identifying the cause of a hearing problem is vital! Children with Down syndrome often have fluctuating hearing loss. When fluid is present, hearing is affected; as fluid drains, hearing improves. This problem means that the child may not consistently hear well. Even though he usually follows directions, he may not follow them on a day when he is experiencing fluctuating hearing loss.

3) A child that experiences pain in the ear or fluid in the middle ear may not hear instructions.

4) Recognize that these health problems left untreated may greatly affect a child's ability to read and succeed in any academic or social setting.

5) Aggressive diagnosis and treatment of any potential medical condition is imperative to student success.

AUTHOR'S INSTRUCTIONAL SUGGESTIONS

1) Identify previous health conditions. Obtain and review the Health Care Guidelines for Individuals with Down Syndrome: 1999 Revision.[2] This document provides the most up-to-date synopsis of children's health care issues and areas of concerns. Discuss surgeries, medications and/or ongoing treatments. Side effects of medications can affect the child's ability to listen and follow directions.

2) Schedule the most challenging academic areas in the morning. Down syndrome along with any accompanying health condition may significantly affect the student's daily stamina. Recall a time when you were asked to face a complex situation on your job after you had been up all night with a new baby, a sick child, or perhaps studying. You can't think! A child with Down syndrome may become more easily tired as the school day progresses. Tiredness significantly increases the time required to process

information and directions.

3) Be aware that the degree of tiredness directly corresponds to behavior. The more tired the child with Down syndrome becomes, the more frustrating the day's challenges become, and the more automatic the negative responses. Analyze perceived behavior problems! Inappropriate physical behavior such as pushing or hitting may reflect a physical inability to process frustrations appropriately rather than a behavior problem.

4) Recognize field trips, field days, holiday activities, or parties as physically and emotionally draining events for a child with Down syndrome. Avoid situations that set the child up for failure. For instance, consider an early release for the student after a morning field trip. A reduction in processing ability may result in academic noncompliance or inappropriate social behavior as the day progresses. The child with Down syndrome does not want to respond improperly. He simply may not have the energy to think a problem through.

5) Realize that unusual behaviors and/or situational responses, i.e., putting head down, crying, and resisting instruction may signal an oncoming illness.

   - A significant change in behavior may be the only indication of an oncoming illness.

   - Some children with Down syndrome have exceedingly high pain thresholds. For example, strep throat may be well developed in a child who is unable to recognize symptoms.

   - Often the child with Down syndrome may be quite ill prior to the onset of recognizable physical signs such as of fever or vomiting.

   - Children with Down syndrome may not know how to

communicate the abstract feelings of a sore throat, nausea, dizziness, or chills.

6) Request that parents alert teachers when their child has not had enough sleep, is overly tired, or is experiencing significant changes at home. The student with Down syndrome requires extra processing time. Any factor that places additional stress on the student will detract from the child's ability to solve problems.

7) Provide for independent learning and social experiences on "overly tired" days. Accept the statement, "I just can't think." It may be true. Read a book to the student or provide time for silent reading to permit the student some down time. Should the student be excessively tired, he may simply not be able to handle demanding academic tasks. Be creative.

8) A child with Down syndrome may require additional recovery time from an illness. Provide adequate recovery periods prior to a return to school. Participation in recess, for example, immediately following a return to school, may further reduce stamina and jeopardize completion of attempted work. Consider an indoor recess for silent reading.

- Realize the initial absence of symptoms following an illness such as fever or cough may not correlate with the child's stamina recovery.

- If you notice a set time of day when the child complains of being tired or seems unable to complete assignments, you may want to plan for a 10 minute rest period. Academic instruction may resume following the planned rest period.

- Suggest to school administration, personnel, nurses, and nurses aides that documentation of chronic medical conditions by the child's physician be considered in attendance policies.

How Do I Talk about Down Syndrome?[10]

We must sometimes remind ourselves to communicate about children with Down syndrome in a positive and accurate manner. The following suggestions may help in that effort.

Good Words to Use:

Baby/Child/Person with Down syndrome – The emphasis should always be on the person first, not the disability. When we take care to put children first and let the disability remain in the background, we are teaching others where the emphasis needs to be.

Developmentally Delayed – This term is the common reference to describe delays in development, such as language, walking, and all other areas of a child's learning process. Most families find it much less offensive than the term *mentally retarded*.

Has Down syndrome – Someone who has Down syndrome is not a *victim of*, *diseased by*, nor do they *suffer from* or are they *afflicted with* Down syndrome. They simply *have* Down syndrome.

Mental Retardation – This term is accurate to describe developmental functioning level but is less acceptable to many parents than the term "developmentally delayed." Use it with caution. A newer, emerging term is "intellectually disabled."

Typically Developing/Non–Disabled Child – Both of these terms are acceptable and positive ways to refer to people who do not have Down syndrome or another disability.

Poor Word Choices:

A Down(s) – A person with Down syndrome is not the disability.

[3]UPS for DownS. How Do I Talk about Down Syndrome? Des Plaines: UPS for DownS, 1996.

There are many other descriptions that should, and do, define that person. It is dehumanizing and strips people of their dignity to be referred to as a disability. Instead of saying "He is a Down syndrome" or "She is Downs," try "He or she *has* Down syndrome."

Down syndrome Child/Baby – This terminology focuses first on the disability rather than on the child. This common misstatement causes parents to cringe, at least inwardly.

Normal Kids – Please realize that we perceive our children as being pretty normal kids. Comparing them to *normal* children implies that a child with Down syndrome is something less than normal.

Retard/Retarded – The best reference is *developmentally delayed* (for children) and *developmentally disabled* (for adults).

Mongolism or Mongoloid – As most of us know, this extremely outdated term once referred to people with Down syndrome. This insulting word should **never** be used when referring to or about someone with Down syndrome.

"They" as in "they are so loving; they smile all the time; they are always happy." – Please don't generalize about people with Down syndrome. "They" are not all alike; nor are people with Down syndrome "eternal children."

"How mild/severe is it?" – A person either has Down syndrome or does not. Down syndrome is not an illness. Having Down syndrome does not mean a person is sick.

"But you're so young!" – Although the chances of a woman having a child with Down syndrome increase significantly over the age of 35, there are far more children with Down syndrome born to younger mothers – they are having more babies.

Handicapped – The proper term would be "has a disability".

Downs or Down's syndrome – There is no "s" or " 's" in the name of this syndrome.

Suffers from/Afflicted with Down syndrome – Our children are not *suffering* or *afflicted*. We must instill a sense of pride and self-esteem in all children to ensure that we do not make anyone feel that Down syndrome is something terrible to be ashamed about.

AUTHOR'S ADDITIONAL COMMENTS

Chapter Six has been included as a guide to remind ourselves of "How often misused words generate misleading thoughts." (Herbert Spencer 1820–1903). As professionals, friends or family, we must communicate about children with Down syndrome in a positive, accurate and informative manner.[10]

AUTHOR'S INSTRUCTIONAL SUGGESTIONS

1) Remember, you have only one opportunity to make a first impression. Your knowledge of, perception of, and interest in a student with Down syndrome will be reflected in the words with which you communicate.

   The parent's first impression of the educator will directly affect all future parental expectations for success or failure of the child's educational experience.

2) Avoid using words that are hurtful or offensive and gently correct those who do so. Uninformed comments of strangers are difficult enough, but when uttered by professionals, the people our children interact with on a daily basis, offensive comments can be heartbreaking and terrifically disappointing.[10]

Summarizing the NDSS Educational Challenges Inclusion Study [6]

In October of 1996, the National Down Syndrome Society (NDSS) completed a study on inclusion "to determine the success or lack of success of inclusive practices, and to survey national trends in inclusion programs for children with Down syndrome." Participation in the study was voluntary and included both parents of children with Down syndrome and teachers. Over 320 questionnaires were mailed to parents and their children's teachers (grades pre-kindergarten through 12th grade). There were 125 parent responses and 120 teacher responses. The findings are summarized in the next pages for the following:

Programming Outcomes on Parent Perceptions of Success

Teacher Perception of Classroom Management Instructional and Behavioral Strategies

Learning Characteristics of Students with Down syndrome

Recommendations for Practitioners

Concluding Remarks

[6]Adapted from National Down Syndrome Society. The Educational Challenges Inclusion Study for the National Down Syndrome Society. New York: NDSS, 1996.

Programming Outcomes on Parent Perceptions of Success[6]

The parent study was designed to obtain write-in responses detailing parents' expectations, prior experience with inclusion, the transition process, their opinions of the professionals involved and their child's adjustment to the process. Parents also rated how successful they felt inclusion was for their child in the following areas: academic gains, socialization, independence, language, self-esteem and the development of friendships.

Factors found to account for the differences in parents who reported successful inclusion experiences as compared to parents who reported unsuccessful inclusion experiences:

- Teacher style with the child (as rated by parents)

- Initial easy placement experience (as compared to problematic first experience)

- Unity between special education and regular education personnel

- Formation of friendships within the class

The four factors above accounted for 43% of the difference in responses between successful and unsuccessful experiences, which indicates highly statistically significant and reliable results. These four factors were present in inclusion experiences that were rated as successful by parents and not found in unsuccessful experiences.

While the teaching arrangement did not affect the parent report of successful inclusion, teacher preparation and style were significant contributors to successful inclusion. Parents stated that they preferred teachers who 1) treated them with respect, 2) had high expectations for the child with Down syndrome, and 3) were willing to modify classroom materials as needed.

The variable with the highest degree of relationship with successful inclusion was the format of the curriculum in the classroom. Teachers who were flexible with the type of student participation and who could alter their use of materials to be more concrete in nature for "hands-on" activities were reported to be highly successful catalysts of achievement for students with Down syndrome.

Corroboration between special education and regular education personnel was a highly predictive factor of parent perception of success. Also, when parents reported a smooth, productive placement process, they found the inclusion experience successful. Those parents who had difficulty with the initial placement reported less satisfaction with the inclusion experience. It seems that first contact impressions tend to set up parent expectations for success or failure.

Parents who reported their children had friends in class also rated the inclusion experience as most successful. This supports the research and anecdotal information that stresses the importance to parents that children have friends in the educational environment. Parents stated that they were pleased to have their children join socially in both formal (sports, dances, birthday parties) and informal (play groups) activities.

To summarize, parental perception of successful inclusion relied on the factors of initial placement experience, teacher style with the child, the format of the curriculum, the unity between special and regular education, confidence in professionals and formation of friendships within class. Teacher preparation should be increased and include areas of communication skills, curricular modifications, and guidelines for working with special educators. This information would suggest that it would be prudent to prepare teachers for skillful curricular design that includes visual cues and performance (concrete) activities, as well as education of the learning styles of students with Down syndrome.

[6]Adapted from National Down Syndrome Society. The Educational Challenges Inclusion Study for the National Down Syndrome Society. New York: NDSS, 1996.

AUTHOR'S ADDITIONAL COMMENTS

Special education is a service not a placement.[9] It is the child's general education classroom that receives support from the special education program. A successful inclusion experience may hinge on the child's initial placement.

The selection of the inclusion teacher, the development of the curriculum, and the selection of a peer group are instrumental in ensuring success. While curriculum for the regular education student is determined by the school district, the curriculum for the special education student is determined by the student. This curriculum is expressed in the IEP. What makes special education so special is that we can design a program specifically to meet the unique, individual needs of each student.[9] **Remember, if a child fails in a program designed just for him, then it may be time to reevaluate the program.** Depending on student progress, case conferences should be convened as needed to revise and update an IEP.

The single most important factor in selecting a teacher is the teacher's desire and comfort in working with a child with Down syndrome. Teachers should be entitled to make a choice to participate in or decline an inclusion experience. This choice should be respected.

A comprehensive IEP should be designed to help the student belong and grow in every environment. The IEP should include a plan to educate student peers about Down syndrome.

AUTHOR'S INSTRUCTIONAL SUGGESTIONS

1) Know thyself. Be honest about the children you feel comfortable within your classroom and your interest in working with a child who has educational challenges. Meeting the individual needs of a child with educational challenges is not easy. It requires more time and effort from the teacher. In return, however, the teacher will experience perhaps the greatest teaching rewards of his career. A

child's success wrapped in smiles and progress are worth the effort.

2) The match between teacher interest, skill, and flexibility is critical to a successful inclusion experience. The teacher must be a willing learner. He/she must

- Learn to learn from the child
- Learn to adapt to student cues (rather than expecting the child to respond and adapt to the teacher)
- Learn how the child learns best, such as visual or auditory, and plan remediation for weaker learning modalities
- Design and utilize materials to maximize learning
- Recognize ineffective or inappropriate instruction
- Be willing to change approaches
  Identify what to teach that will be both useful and meaningful to the child
- Modify curriculum to meet student needs
- Learn how to apply developmental, behavioral, and educational principles to the individual child[9]

3) Utilize and revise the IEP. A team, including the parents who best know the special needs of the child, has carefully developed it. The child's educational program needs to be designed and implemented to ensure integration of skill development throughout the inclusion program. Skills targeted during speech and occupational therapy must be reviewed and practiced throughout the day. Skills cannot be taught in isolation. The case conference team is an excellent resource for problem solving strategies.

Students will likely be most fearful or critical of differences they do not understand. The following lesson plan is offered as a way to generate acceptance through education.

Sample Lesson Plan
"An Elementary Understanding
of
Down syndrome"

This approach is targeted for children in the elementary classroom. When presenting this lesson to the class, I prefer the child with Down syndrome be engaged in a different activity outside the class room.

Objective:
To define Down syndrome, to experience how it might feel to have Down syndrome, and to develop an understanding of the importance of friends.

Materials:
- National Down Syndrome Society. <u>Friendship Knows No Boundaries</u>. New York, NDSS.[7]

- A parent of a child who has Down syndrome (my son, Michael in this example).

- A family portrait of the family of the child who has Down syndrome or a picture of each family member.

- A pair of heavy socks, preferably tube socks, for each child in the classroom.[7]

- Two or three new decks of playing cards.[7]

- Student coats or jackets (the need is for zippers, buttons, snaps, hooks, etc.).

- VCR or other props as needed

- "A Friend Like Me" poem. Include a copy for every student.

24

Procedure:

Introduce parent. Have parent seated in front of the children on the floor. Display poster.

> **Parent:** "Thank you so much for having me. I am so excited about today. Does anyone know when Mother's Day is? (May) Today is another Mother's Day for me because I have the chance to share with you what is most important in my life – my family." (other holidays, Grandparents Day, Christmas, Valentine's Day may substitute for Mother's Day.)
>
> "Before I start, I would like you each to do something for me: Stand up, go to your locker, get your coat/jacket, come back in, and sit on top of it."
>
> Display family portrait.
>
> Introduce each member. Tell something about each member. This provides an opportunity for the children to realize that Michael has a family similar to their own.
>
> Point to the picture of Michael and ask, "Do you know who this is? Michael is my very special son." (Every parent should be able to state something their child can do that most people can't such as give special hugs, etc.)
>
> "Did you know that Michael has done something no one in this school has ever done? Actually, I don't know anyone else who has done what Michael has done."
>
> "How many of you have watched the ball drop in New York on New Year's Eve?"
>
> "How many of you have seen the huge television screen in Times Square?"
>
> "Well, Michael is a star."

25

Read letter announcing Michael as one of 200 children selected to have his picture displayed on the Times Square screen in New York city to kick off National Down Syndrome Week.

Show video clip.

"Did you know that you know a real movie star?" (Whatever the child's special skill, this discussion elevates the child in the students' eyes).

"Why would Michael be chosen to kickoff National Down syndrome Week?"

"Who knows what Down syndrome is?" (Many children know that you are born with Down syndrome. Many will state that it is "bad.")

"Please look at each other. Do you each have the same color hair or eyes? Are you the same size?"

"Isn't it great. We are all different. Can you imagine how boring it would be if we were all the same? Well, we may not be the same on the outside, but we must be the same on the inside...no."

Explanation: (The explanation can be general or specific depending on the age group of the class.) "Actually, we are all the same in some ways. We are all made up of cells. The cells hold chromosomes. Chromosomes give us inherited characteristics from our parents."

"What does inherited mean?"

"What kinds of traits can we inherit from parents?" (Eye and skin color, height)

"You all have 23 pairs of chromosomes, or 46 total.

One chromosome in each pair comes from your mother and one chromosome comes from your father."[2]

"But do you know what? Michael is so special, he has more chromosomes. Your cells have 46 but Michael has an extra one giving him 47."

"Isn't that something?"

"That extra chromosome makes Michael my special little boy, and that is the reason he has Down syndrome."

"Do you know I think this extra chromosome helps Michael enjoy you all as friends? Michael doesn't notice if you have a pimple or if you're skinny or heavy. He enjoys almost everyone and everything."

"Down syndrome can also make some activities that Michael wants to do harder."

"Have you ever noticed how Michael runs? Well, children with Down syndrome often have low muscle tone or weaker muscles than we do. His muscles had to learn how to crawl, walk, run."

"Does Michael speak differently from you? His speech is also part of the Down syndrome, low muscle tone, and other reasons."

"Learning is harder for Michael because of Down syndrome."

"Someone asked why Michael was 11 years old in third grade when most 11 year old children are in the fifth grade. Michael is not dumb. He can learn the same kinds of things you learn, but it just takes him longer."

"Do you know how it feels to have Down syndrome?"

(Most answer "bad".)

Pass out a pair of tube socks to each student.

"I would like you to put these socks on your hands, then I'd like you to put your coat/jacket on and zip/snap/button."

"By the way, assume that you have no friends, parents, or teachers available to help. I'll give you three minutes."

When the children say, "I can't do this," tell them, "In my house Michael is not permitted to say I can't. He may only say, I can, help me please."

Immediately a child will say, "But you said we had no friends, parents, or teachers available to help." Needing help that isn't always available is the point.

Call time.

"How many of you found it difficult to fasten your coat with socks on your hands?"

"What would have made it easier?" (Friends.)

Explanation: "From the time Michael gets up until he goes to bed, he has to do everything with the feeling of having socks on his hands because of the low muscle tone. Do you see why Michael might be the last one out to recess? It may not be because he is poking, but because getting ready is harder for him."

"What could you do to help Michael?" (Be a friend.)

"Oh my, you are each so very, very important because you can be a friend and help someone else. That would be really great!"

"Okay, I have another activity for you. Keep the socks on your hands. I need three or four people to be helpers." (Choose students who are in the greatest need to develop understanding). "I'd like you each to pass out five cards to every person."

"I would like each of you to use these cards to build a standing house made from cards. I will give you three minutes. No talking please." (This activity is impossible for most under the best of circumstances.)

Call time.

"What happened?" (Someone usually says, "That was impossible or too hard.")

"That's true. It is almost impossible to build a house of cards. But, you know what, I'm proud of all of you because you tried."

"Some things are actually impossible for Michael; all I ask is that he try."

(Collect socks and playing cards. Make the next part of the activity personal by sharing stories with the children.)

"Now I would like to talk to you about what you like to do."

"How many of you like to ride bikes? Wow, Mike does too."
"How many of you like to play soccer? Michael does too."
(Tailor questions to your specific child.)

"How many of you like to play basketball? Michael does too. If you ever want to watch something really neat, ask Michael to shoot some free throws from the foul line. You will be surprised! Usually he can make about ten baskets before he misses. Michael may not know the rules very well, but he sure is super at foul shots. If you ever want to play with Michael at recess, get a basketball and shoot free throws."

"How many of you like to play baseball? You won't believe this, but Michael does too. Oh, I must tell you. Now we know Michael runs differently, but if you ever have the bases loaded and you want to bring in three runs, put Michael at bat. My, oh my, can he hit! Michael has never made it past first base because running is hard, but he is sure to bring in the runs."

"How many of you like to swim? Michael does too. As a matter of fact, Michael is an excellent swimmer. He probably swims better than many of us. He would really enjoy swimming with you."

"Gracious, you like to do the same things Michael does."

"Michael may play a little bit differently, but there are some things he can do very well...just like you."

Explanation: "Children with Down syndrome have the same likes and dislikes that you do. They like the same music, the same movies and the same clothing. Just like you, they enjoy having friends. You can have a close and special friendship with a classmate who has Down syndrome.[9]

"He may need your help with schoolwork or his coat or boots, and that will make you feel good because you can help a friend. There are times when your friend with Down syndrome can help you. Remember, true friendship knows no boundaries. (Show NDSS Poster)

"Now, I'd like to ask how many of you have grandparents?"

"How many of you love your grandparents?"

"How many of you have or know a grandparent that you love that has had a stroke?"

"What is a stroke?"

"Does someone who has had a stroke have any trouble using a hand or leg the way they used to?"

"Does the person that has had the stroke talk differently?"

"Now, you have a grandparent you love who has had a stroke and that paralyzed their arm or leg. Perhaps it is difficult for them to talk."

"Do you love them any less?" (No.)

"Are they dumb now? I mean they don't talk the same." (No.)

"Of course, your grandparent is not dumb and I'm certain that you love as much or more than you did before."

Explanation: "Some of you have asked why Michael talks funny, or runs funny, or writes funny. Well, that is because he has Down syndrome. That is just the way he was made."

"But you know what? He is not dumb and I love him just like you love a grandparent who has been changed because of a stroke."

"Before I go, I have a gift for each of you. (Distribute poem, A Friend Like Me.)

"This is a very special poem that means a lot to me. Before I read it, I need to know what the words rigid and obstacle mean." (Discuss.)

Read poem.

"This is my gift to you, and since this has been my Mother's Day, I would like a gift from you too. Does anyone know what that might be?" (Be a friend to Michael.)

"Oh my, you have all been wonderful. You are very good listeners. Thank you so much for sharing yourselves with me. You have given me a fantastic Mother's Day!"

A Friend Like Me
By Tracey Sandrock

Please don't be afraid of me
I want to be your friend.
And if you get to know me
Your rigid thoughts might bend.

Thoughts that I am different
From others that you know.
I really am no different
And this I'd like to show.

I live and breathe and laugh and cry
I love to play and learn.
I sometimes do things differently
Which can cause some concern.

You see, some say I'm special
I guess this much is true,
But if you were to ask me
I'd say you're special, too.

We're all a little different
No two are just the same.
It's really something wonderful
That way there is no blame.

When things don't go just perfectly
And others get confused.
And say things like "poor child"
And other terms they use.

It's okay if you look at me
And might not understand.
It's okay if you touch me
And even hold my hand.

My life has many obstacles
Much more than you could know.
But that's not what I dwell on
I'm me, that's all, and so...

Please don't be afraid of me
I want you just to see.
How truly great and wonderful
A friend like me can be.

Teacher Perception of Classroom Management Instructional and Behavioral Strategies[6]

The teacher study was designed using write-in responses, rating scales (of 1-5), and checklists to elicit information detailing their prior experience and expectations, training and preparation, behavior management, and classroom operations, instructional curriculum, and attitudes toward inclusion. Teachers also rated the inclusion experience on how much extra work was required and how it related to their expectations.

The most common teaching arrangement, or inclusion model, entailed the regular teacher working with one additional inclusion aide (87% of the cases), whose responsibilities included one-on-one tutorial with the child with Down syndrome and whole class assistance. The inclusion aide stays with the child from year to year. Teachers report that this arrangement provides stability with programming instruction.

The best learning arrangements reported were one-on-one and small group instruction. Peer tutors, computers and team teaching were found to be sometimes effective. Large groups and the whole class were reported not effective at all for students with Down syndrome. The most effective instructional location was reported to be the student's desk area.

Concrete or "hands-on" materials were reported the most effective for instruction of students with Down syndrome. The computer, paper and pencil tasks, and textbooks were sometimes effective (only in the upper grades). Workbooks were not found to be useful because most workbooks are heavily dependent on language comprehension (a problem area for students with Down syndrome) or have too many distractions, or problems on a page, both of which are confusing and overwhelming. While the regular education teacher and inclusion aide were reported as the most effective instructors for the child, 44% of the teachers also wrote that

[6]Adapted from National Down Syndrome Society. The Educational Challenges Inclusion Study for the National Down Syndrome Society. New York: NDSS, 1996.

peers were extremely effective instructional agents.

Teachers felt that homework was important for the student with Down syndrome because it helped to bridge the gap between home and school, reinforce concepts discussed in class, and inform parents about what a student is learning.

Teachers did not have to modify their behavior management systems for adequate class control due to the addition of a student with Down syndrome. Children with Down syndrome responded to the same behavior management techniques as the rest of the class. Teachers reported that praise was the best behavior management strategy. Material rewards, time out, peer pressure, loss of privilege, and contact with parents was sometimes helpful. Ignoring, reprimands, and punishment were not effective at all, possibly because a student with Down syndrome might not link these consequences with his/her inappropriate behavior.

49% of teachers reported that inclusion caused extra work in the areas of modifying homework, class assignments, tests, and grading procedures and necessitated more contact with the parent. Teachers evaluated students with Down syndrome on their efforts and participation in class rather than primarily through tests or homework. Threat of lower grades was an ineffective motivator for students with Down syndrome to work harder and try their best. Teachers desired more one-on-one individual instructional time, more planning time, and more information on learning characteristics of children with Down syndrome.

Additional Findings[6]

Anecdotal parent comments from the study provided additional useful information along four major themes:

- Teacher personalities make or break the inclusion experience.
  The match of the regular education teacher's personality to the child is crucial to having asuccessful year. Parents reported that principals selected the inclusion teachers individually and carefully. Many parents also reported difficulty in communicating, coordinating, and sharing responsibility between special education and regular education personnel.

- Communication between school personnel and parents is necessary for success.
  Parents who were more involved and had better communication felt much better about their child's inclusion experience. In addition, teachers received most of their pertinent information about children from parents. Daily notebooks were reported as being an invaluable asset for communication.

- Classmates often make up for any shortcomings of the staff.
  Although most parents reported that their child's inclusion aide was the professional who worked best with their child, 33% of the parents preferred not to have an aide present. These parents felt that aides tend to help with everything, which isolates and stigmatizes the child. Aides can also cause other kids to shy away from the child with Down syndrome. Both parents and teachers felt positive about the use of peer tutors in class. Many teachers of sixth grade and higher reported that peer intervention worked better than teacher assistance.

- A balance should be struck between the developmental needs of students and chronological advancement.
  The discrepancy between slower development and chronological needs of students with Down syndrome

as compared to their typical peers is not as apparent in pre-school or kindergarten, where the children assimilate more easily, but becomes more apparent when higher academic expectations are set for the elementary years and upper grades. Many parents and teachers reported difficulty in this area.

This balance is the crucial aspect of inclusion, having students learn with their chronologically aged peers when their developmental needs are different. Parents who reported successful inclusion describe their children's teachers as positive motivators who foster independence and self-reliance. The majority of teachers allowed their students with Down syndrome to remain with the peer group but modified the curriculum with less expectation for mastery of detail, and concepts and retention of learning.

[6]Adapted from National Down Syndrome Society. The Educational Challenges Inclusion Study for the National Down Syndrome Society. New York: NDSS, 1996.

AUTHOR'S ADDITIONAL COMMENTS

Everything you want to be learned must be taught.[7] An elaboration of some of the study findings, I believe, will be helpful in assisting the educator to effectively apply the data in the classroom.

Teaching Arrangement

1) One-on-one instruction is essential for the comprehension of challenging academic instruction. However, it is the blend of learning center services and inclusion experiences that will best meet students' needs.

2) "The best learning arrangements reported were one-on-one and small group." Further support is shown through the finding, "Large groups and whole class settings were reported not effective at all for students with Down syndrome."[4] I believe these statements refer to the most

effective location for academic instruction. Independence, language development, and self-esteem increase when other classmates are used as role models. The child with Down syndrome must be viewed as a "whole" child with both social and academic needs.

Instructional Materials and Aides

1) Children with Down syndrome may be easily distracted. Without careful planning and preparation, initial experiences with concrete or "hands-on" materials may turn into unwanted play sessions. Use body parts for initial concrete math experiences, i.e., place a sticker on one fist and a sticker on the other fist (1 sticker plus 1 sticker equals what?). As these materials have limited play value, the concept remains the focus of instruction.[12]

2) Caution should be taken in using peer tutors and computers as instructional agents. Computers and peer tutors afford opportunities for the student with Down syndrome to practice and learn errors. Computers and peer tutors are best utilized as tools for reinforcement and review of mastered materials. Once a student with Down syndrome has acquired an incorrect skill, "unlearning" and reteaching are extremely difficult.

3) Plan for free exploration of commercial materials such as pattern blocks or math manipulatives prior to academic instruction in order to decrease play value.

4) "*Workbooks were not found to be useful.*"[4] Traditionally, commercial workbooks have not met the needs of students with Down syndrome. More useful and innovative materials keep the visual field (ground) plain, reduce the number of pictures per page, remove framing, reduce the amount of text per page, and reduce the amount of new material presented with each page. Appropriate materials must decrease the amount of visual distractions on a page, which are confusing and overwhelming for a student with Down syndrome.

5) The visual presentation of instructional materials alone may determine a lesson's outcome. Imagine that your high school child brings you a homework assignment with forty-four chemistry equations to be completed. I, for one, can feel my chest tighten. It is not that you cannot assist your child, but the visual text is overwhelming. Had you been presented with one problem or one row of equations, your panic level would have been lower. Students with Down syndrome typically possess a decreased academic threshold. An overwhelming amount of text on a page may create a visual obstacle unrelated to the task.

6) Lessons should be designed to provide highly structured, meaningful experiences from simple to complex.

7) The success level directly corresponds to the percent of new material presented with respect to the percent of familiar material. Material can only be deemed familiar if you have presented it at a prior time. Students with Down syndrome can be passive learners. Never assume![12]

8) Initially, I recommend the introduction of 5% new material imposed upon 95% familiar material. The level of success should determine the rate of new skill introduction. If the student succeeds 80% of the time, the pacing and skill are appropriate. The ultimate objective is to present 15% new material on 85% familiar material.[12]

Instructional techniques

1) The student with Down syndrome requires tight, structured routines. Tight structure decreases uncertainty in the learning task, decreases frustration, and advances the learning significantly.

2) Model, model, model. For example, if a student is expected to come into a room and sit down quietly, then he must be taught how to walk into the room and sit down quietly. You cannot assume the student knows how to do

this task without being taught.[12]

3) The student should also be given a clear, consistent calendar of daily routines for each subject. Holding to anticipated routines reduces task resistance.

4) Alterations in learned routines may be upsetting to a child with Down syndrome. Substitute teachers must be aware of practices and routines specific to the student with Down syndrome.

5) Students with Down syndrome may experience the "first day back" syndrome when returning to school following an extended illness. The first day back may be a difficult day for the student. Learned routines have been broken. It may take at least one day for the student to readjust. Be patient.

6) Children with Down syndrome appear to be highly sensitive and responsive to pacing (teacher established rate at which students work). These students seem to require faster, tighter pacing than some other students. It is critical that the student be encouraged to "work fast." While the child may initially need more processing time, pacing definitely increases the student's rate of success by eliminating opportunities for distraction and minimizing "failure" opportunities. Although this approach is contradictory to some current thinking, fast pacing is an effective method for enhancing student progress. Ask your students to "work fast." **The goal is not to teach the child with Down syndrome to be slow.** When we slow the student down, we allow for mental intrusion and subsequently teach the wrong behavior.[12]

7) Pacing should include a consistent amount of material every session, for example "three pages of writing or math" per session. Reducing the uncertainty of work volume reduces resistant behaviors.[12]

8) Students with Down syndrome appear to require many trials for the content to be learned. The student may tire of the content, however, and switching to distributed practice (ongoing content review dispersed over time) may help maintain the intensity of learning.

9) It is essential that the mastery of one specific academic area (i.e., complete alphabet recognition prior to sight word instruction) not be required prior to introducing other academic areas. Curricular areas must be presented simultaneously and overlapped in order to allow for progress in areas of ability while review continues to occur in more frustrating areas.

10) When starting a new task, the student with Down syndrome may show resistant behavior, "No, I don't want to.," head down. This response may be due to lack of situational processing (assimilating assignment expectations) by the student. It is most effective to permit the student to have processing (thinking) time, i.e., **WAIT for the student to begin!**[12] This waiting time may be 5 minutes or longer. Frequent positive reinforcement should be used to move the student closer to the desired behavior. A typical reinforcement sequence could be: He looks at his pencil. "Good." He touches his pencil. "Good, you are getting ready to work. Let's begin." Additionally, the task may need to be adjusted based upon observation. **Removing the student from the task by using a "time out" technique is not effective.** In doing this, the teacher inadvertently reinforces the resistant behavior.

11) Be certain to incorporate behavioral expectations into clear, concise directions. "You may begin working, stay in your seat please." With avoidance or resistant behavior, add, "I will wait for you to begin." Be patient. You may need to train yourself to remain calm rather than reacting with anger or frustration. There should be no further talking during the wait time. Talking will result in a power struggle or negotiations; simply wait. The student is expected to

stay at his workspace. Allowing the student to state he is tired and remove himself to a rest area will also reinforce resistant behavior.

12) Train yourself to state clear concise directions one time. Reduce teacher talking.[12] Children with Down syndrome are highly sensitive to intruding noise. Unnecessary repeating and talking are one more source of distraction.[7]

13) Be flexible to the specific needs and characteristics of a child with Down syndrome, such as health considerations, stamina, breaks in routine, and adjustments to new social demands. Create a success-oriented atmosphere.

Behavior

It is important that the teacher be a clinician of student behaviors. The teacher should analyze and diagnose behavioral responses with respect to the learning characteristics of the student with Down syndrome. The child with Down syndrome will need more frequent encouragement and positive feedback than the average learner. He will also need an accepting environment in which he can feel free to make mistakes and attempt to become more independent. The principle should always be: "It is better to try and fail than not to try at all!"

THE GOAL: Slow, steady, positive progress

1) Success is the key to behavior management. Design your classroom and instruction for success.

2) Special care must be given to all directions for every activity. Directions must be clear, concise, and considerate of delayed language concepts. If a student is disruptive, it could be that they are not processing the language of the lesson. If the directions state, for example, "Ring the correct answer," rather than "Circle the correct answer," language may inhibit compliance. Sometimes, using a visual aid can help to convey the concept.

3) Directions should include expected behavior, such as "Begin working; no talking please" or "Begin working; stay in your seat please." The inclusion of expected behavior in directions eliminates reprimand for unwanted behaviors once work has begun.[7] This technique is magically effective. (It works beautifully with teenagers also!)

4) Praise is absolutely the best behavior management technique and motivator.

5) Reward correct responses immediately to ensure that students are associating the reward with what was correctly done.

6) At each new task level, the rate of positive feedback should be 100%, item by item. Positive feedback is utilized with each new task level and reduced to line-by-line, then page-by-page, with the ultimate goal being independence on that task. Using this approach can make progress slower; however, the progress should occur steadily with less resistance.[12]

7) **All reinforcement should be positive.** Even if the response appears incorrect, all productive efforts are praised as good.[12]

8) There are no right/wrong, correct/incorrect, or good/bad activities. No effort is wrong. All reinforcement is designed to move the student's work closer to the goal of mastery. Ongoing remodeling and encouragement are essential to student progress.[12]

9) Phrases such as, "No, that's wrong;" "No, let me show you;" or "That's not right," should never be used. There is only one word to be used during student sessions: "Good" plus remodeling as necessary.[12]

10) Reward independence.

11) The memory game is an effective means to teach desired behaviors.[12] Identify desired behavior, i.e., to eliminate pushing, shoving, rough play. State clearly and concisely, i.e., "No touch." Rather than discussing and restating the undesired behavior focus on the desired behavior. Ask the student daily, "Did you remember to play the Memory Game?" "What did you remember?" "No touch." Be sure to remind the child of the Memory Game prior to known behavior provoking situations such as lunch, recess, or bathroom use.[12]

12) Avoidance behaviors reflect the student's level of fear of failure and/or frustration. Always acknowledge student feelings with "I understand. Let's try anyhow." or "I know. We can work together." Frequently, merely acknowledging anxieties allows the child with Down syndrome to begin to work.

13) Consult the parents to determine meaningful consequences for unwanted behavior. Checks on the board, loss of stickers, loss of recess, or threat of a lower grade may be meaningless and ineffective. Occasionally, the most unique consequence is the most significant. My son, Michael, is shattered when his "hot dog" or a favorite movie is withheld. He is expected to earn these privileges by using good behavior at school.

14) Always ask the child with Down syndrome, "Why?" When the student reacts or behaves in an unexpected or an unusual manner, ask why. The reasons may be quite surprising and may make complete sense to the student. For instance, I received a call from school one day explaining that for some reason Michael had taken his shirt off and was bare-chested after recess. "Why?" He had gotten a drink. A drop of water had gotten on his shirt, and, because of increased tactile sensitivity, he was completely intolerant of the wet spot.

15) Unacceptable physical behaviors must be interrupted and halted immediately. The consequence must be significant enough to stop physical pushing, shoving or any other physical outburst. A teacher suggested to me once that Michael simply needed to push more gently. Michael does not understand degrees of pushing. He may not push, period! Undesirable physical behavior is unacceptable and may result in injuries or suspensions.

16) Consistency is essential to behavior modification. Never use empty threats.

17) All persons in contact with a student expressing inappropriate behaviors must be aware of the agreed upon behavior plan, i.e., teachers, learning center teachers, lunch monitors, and recess monitors. Threatened consequences from a myriad of different people will not alter behavior and may reinforce and escalate it.

18) Define friendship to the peers of a child with Down syndrome: "Being a friend means being honest." Peers need to tell another child when they do not like what that child is doing.

19) Of utmost importance is to remember that a child with Down syndrome is a child first! Behavioral expectations should be the same for all children. It is unacceptable to permit objectionable behaviors with excuses, such as, "You need to understand, Jimmy has Down syndrome." This attitude is detrimental to the child and his future social success.

Learning Characteristics of Students with Down Syndrome[6]

To better understand how students with Down syndrome learn, the NDSS study examines six areas:

Attention
Memory
Concept attainment
Mediational strategies
Transfer of learning
Motivation

Attention[6]

Attention represents the ability of an individual to focus on a specific item in a task. It can be broken down into two stages:

- Stage 1 – the ability to attend (to focus and stay on task for a period of time, i.e., attention span), and

- Stage 2 – the ability to identify and process relevant material and respond appropriately.

A child who is developmentally disabled generally has a lower capacity to pay attention. Increasing the student's attention span and the ability to identify relevant information is essential for all further learning. Once the student has mastered the appropriate attention span and has identified the relevant stimulus, he can be expected to learn the task and perform as well as the typically performing student.

Suggestions for Classroom Practice[6]

1) Present stimuli or objects that have clear and obvious dimension and vary as few dimensions as possible (e.g., color and size or texture). Otherwise, the student may be responding to a dimension other than what the teacher is expecting.
2) Use attention-getting techniques such as prompts, cues or lighting. You can even make a secret signal with the student for fun.

3) Placing work on a different background color or texture may enhance attention.

4) Remove extraneous distracting stimuli such as pictures on walls, or too many problems on a page. Do not place the student next to a window, door, or high traffic area.

5) Reward correct responses immediately to ensure that students are associating the reward to what was correctly done.

[6]Adapted from National Down Syndrome Society. The Educational Challenges Inclusion Study for the National Down Syndrome Society. New York: NDSS, 1996.

AUTHOR'S ADDITIONAL COMMENTS

Attention skills are the foundation for all learning. To increase the child's attention span, eliminate distractions, isolate the task, and program instruction.[7]

It cannot be assumed that prerequisite learning skills—such as, attention, memory, language development, auditory, enhanced work rate (pacing), ability to follow directions, discrimination, and tracking, exist or are developing at a natural rate. These learning skills are all required for the successful understanding of academic materials. Although these skills usually develop naturally in most typical learners, we can **never assume** that children with special education needs will passively develop such learning skills without **specific** training. This training is founded in the principle that everything you want to be learned must be taught![12]

When training the student with Down syndrome to improve attention skills, you need to recognize that the child with limited attention skills will also be more vulnerable to environmental distractions. Here is the educational starting point.

The environment must be as distraction free as possible.[12] Imagine attempting to prepare your yearly taxes while seated at a card table near the checkout lanes in Wal-mart. Unimaginable! Easily distracted students must feel this way when seated in a classroom that suffers from "perceptual indigestion" created by a well-intending teacher. An inability to

47

pay attention is heightened by a multitude of displays, i.e., butterflies hanging from the ceiling, walls abounding with student artwork.

The physical positioning of desks will also influence the child's ability to pay attention. Organizing desks into social clusters will result in social behavior. Is it reasonable to ask a student to hold a picture and not look at it?[7] Is it reasonable to arrange desks in social pods and expect no socializing? Could four teachers sit in a group without talking an entire day or even an hour?[12]

To decrease unwanted behaviors of children with lower attention skills, it is the educator's obligation to carefully manage the physical dynamics of the classroom environment.

AUTHOR'S INSTRUCTIONAL SUGGESTIONS

1) Prior to other academic instruction, program the child's learning to target attention skills.[12]

2) Research attention skill instruction programs. Investigate programs, such as, the Werhli Fitness Program.[12] This program specifically trains a child in learning performance skills including attention, discrimination, memory, language development, and pacing.[12]

3) Display student artwork on bulletin boards at the back of the room, hang art projects from the ceiling in the hall, cover open bookcases, utilize linear arrangement of student desks.[12]

4) Recognize that a student experiencing too much stimulation may tend to withdraw and seek a "timeout" (escape) away from the problem environment. Students may state, "I want to sleep," "I need to go for a walk," "I need to go home." These responses can easily happen during times of over-stimulation, for example, at parties or large group gatherings. It is simply an overwhelming environment.

5) Train attention skills.[7] Utilize tapes and books, lessons with empty content with time on task as the goal. When training attention skills with the goal of increasing an attention span, do not introduce new material.[12]

6) Identify and isolate the targeted skill. The teaching of an academic skill can often interfere with the progress of a performance skill. For example, when specifically training attention skills, errors in math, reading, or letter identification should not take precedence over the attention training objectives. An academic skill should not become a barrier if increased attention span is the goal. Remember the goal![12]

7) Provide a balance of attention skill training with academic training in all learning modalities, i.e., written, visual, auditory.[12]

8) Increase pacing (student work rate) to hold attention.[12]

Memory

Memory is the ability to store and retrieve (upon demand) previously experienced sensations and perceptions, even when the stimulus that originally evoked them is no longer present. There are two types of memory.

1) Short-term memory – As information passes through a student's senses, it impacts short-term memory, which is heavily based on language labels. A language label is a name for an object or action. A typical student's short-term memory is generally limited to five to nine pieces of information, which lasts from 30 seconds to a couple of minutes.

2) Long-term memory – To store information into long-term memory, an individual must mentally interact with the material through behavior or experience or through the use of a memory strategy. These strategies can be either spontaneously applied, as in the case of someone with a

good memory, or improved by training, as in the case of someone with a poor memory. Long-term memory comes from meaningful impressions or relationships, which can last a lifetime.

Individuals with Down syndrome tend to have poor memory for three reasons: 1) Language delays create a disadvantage in acquiring language labels for short-term memory; 2) Children with Down syndrome tend to have a limited repertoire of memory strategies; 3) Students with Down syndrome tend to be "inactive" learners when it comes to memory.

Suggestions for Classroom Practice

1) Use labeling or verbal associations to make up for any language deficits related to memory and learning. Use smaller clusters of information and sequence ideas.

2) Repeat and practice skills to promote learning.

3) Select interesting and meaningful tasks which individuals will enjoy repeating.

4) Teach the learner to use rehearsal strategies and practice them.

5) Provide opportunities to practice skills in many contexts and use multisensory approaches, involving hands-on activities.

6) Show patterns in things to be memorized and teach more sophisticated memory tricks.

AUTHOR'S ADDITIONAL COMMENTS

As stated in the NDSS study, individuals with Down syndrome tend to have poor memory for three reasons. Elaboration of these three points follows.

1) Children with Down syndrome are at a disadvantage for short-term memory due to language delays. Without language labels, comprehending and storing information is impossible. Foreign language study is a perfect example. As students commence language study, they are required to engage in massive memorization. Without a language label base, communication cannot occur. Comprehension without labels can actually be summed up by the popular, humorous statement, "It's Greek to me." What has been said is foreign and makes no sense!

2) Individuals with Down syndrome are also passive or "inactive" learners. You can never expect that labels have been learned coincidentally. For example, my son came home with homework from his speech teacher: "Could you please help him learn the meaning of the words brick, dust pan, and iron?" I was shocked. We live in a brick house, but I had never specifically labeled "brick" for him! Additionally, Michael and I clean our fireplaces weekly with a dustpan and brush, but he never asked and I never thought to label "dust pan." Consequently, he did not know what a dust pan was. Lastly, I completely understood that Michael had no comprehension of "iron." I hate to iron and he may never have seen one! This example taught me that I could never assume that Michael would naturally develop a language base without specific teaching.

3) Finally, because they are passive learners experiencing language delays, children with Down syndrome cannot be expected to have a repertoire of memory strategies without explicit instruction.

Once children with Down syndrome have acquired a language base, however, they can comprehend and remember information and perform as well as their peers.[4] Much like a computer, information must be identified (labeled) and entered (understood) before it can be filed (memory). Newly entered data (short-term memory) can only be retained by a computer if that data is specifically stored and "saved" (long-term memory).

The number of bits (pieces) of information that can be stored refers to the amount of information that can be accepted and stored by the individual.

Information in short-term memory is retained long enough to be put to immediate use. Once used, it is dropped, and memory channels are filled with new information. If the information has future value, we must mentally interact with it so that it can be stored in long-term memory. Information must be used and rehearsed if it is to remain available in long-term memory; otherwise, it will be dropped and replaced.[9]

Computers have limitations in the number of sources of data inputs that can be handled simultaneously (channel capacity). Individuals also have limitations in channel capacity. Channel capacity is determined by the number of new items or bits of information that an individual can retain briefly in their short-term memory. Having an understanding of channel capacity and an awareness of the channel capacity of your child can be a key to programming for her success and is helpful in avoiding mistakes that may set her up for failure.[9]

The general population has an average of seven memory channels, referred to by psychologists as "the Magic Number Seven." For this reason phone numbers have seven digits. If we do not anticipate needing a number at some future time, the number is not placed in our long-term memory and is forgotten. However, if it is our own new phone number or one of a close friend, we write it down, and, in time, with use and practice, it becomes stored in our long-term memory. The number remains in long-term memory as long as it is useful.[9]

People with Down syndrome, however, may have fewer than seven memory channels. Although children in general have fewer memory channels, children with Down syndrome usually have fewer than their peers at any age.[9] When we expect someone with Down syndrome to perform as if he/she has seven channels, when, in fact, he/she may have fewer, performance falters. The child is unsuccessful, becomes frustrated, and may display unwanted behaviors.[9]

The typical test for channel capacity is to ask the child to repeat numbers or non-related words after you, such as: 5, 2; 8, 1, 6; 7, 2, 49; 6, 8, 3, 2, 4. The number of numbers repeated usually suggests the channel capacity and tests auditory memory. It must be remembered that students with Down syndrome are generally visual learners with better visual memory. To test visual memory, pictures, printed words, numbers may be used. For example, a child is shown a picture and then it is removed. The child is asked, "What did you see?" Gradually increase the number of pictures shown. Channel capacity is measured by the number of pictures shown that the child remembers.[9] Although testing measures a child's channel capacity, daily classroom performance should guide day-to-day instruction. Ongoing evaluation is the key to making thoughtful and constructive decisions concerning programming, teaching techniques, and strategies.[9]

Testing gives you an idea of the child's channel capacity, which provides tremendous insight into the percent of new material that a specific child can successfully manage. For instance, a child with five memory channels could not handle seven new sight words per session; nor could the child who performs with three memory channels follow five-step directions.[9]

Children with Down syndrome frequently have auditory deficits. Therefore, both visual and auditory channel testing may be the best predictors of memory channel capacity. It must be remembered, however, that auditory memory deficits can be misinterpreted as behavior problems. Inaccurate perceptions, such as, "I know she knows how to do it; she just ignores me. If I tell her once, I tell her a thousand times. She is so stubborn." are often indicative of this situation. It could be that during the time the directions were stated, they were heard and understood. However, if the spoken word exists for only an instant, a child with Down syndrome, who requires longer to process information and who has decreased short-term memory skills, may only recall the last words in a set of directions. For instance, if the teacher says, "Take your coats off, hang them in the coat closet, get your materials out of your backpack, go into the room, and sit down quietly," the student with Down syndrome may have only remembered the last directions given. The teacher may observe the student with Down syndrome walk to her desk and sit down quietly while holding her backpack. The child may only have remembered the last set of directions. This demonstrates fewer memory channels and difficulty with auditory memory. It does not demonstrate that a child is ignoring a direction or being stubborn. Consider the child's channel capacity when giving directions. A child with Down syndrome may not be able to recall multiple step directions quickly.

The student may also have a longer than expected latency, the lapse of time between the request and the response. In other words, it takes longer for the child to process and respond. Unfortunately, the child may appear to be unwilling to comply when, in reality, he is processing what has been said. For these reasons, clear, concise directions must be given slowly. Writing instructions down or using illustrations may also help the student to remember. After all, that is what we do in our daily planners.[9]

When we give too much unnecessary information, the child must go through yet another difficult process that he may not be able to manage. In addition to hearing, understanding, remembering, retrieving, and responding, we also ask him to "filter" out the irrelevant information and recall only the relevant. This ability to identify the relevant information is the second component of attention skills. Typically, this sorting alone is a difficult process for a child with Down syndrome.

When considering memory channels and the development of language, the child's ability to understand is usually more advanced than his ability to express. This is known as the receptive-expressive gap. Because children with Down syndrome have difficulty with expressive language, teachers may underestimate what they know, understand, and can learn.

Awareness that some children with Down syndrome may have 100% receptive abilities with little (perhaps 50%) expressive skills obligates educators to find and develop appropriate expressive measures of receptive ability such as multiple choice, yes/no, or written discrimination questioning techniques as opposed to narratives or written essays.[4]

Unless the child has a hearing impairment, talking louder does not help a child understand or respond better. When interacting with children with Down syndrome, we often fail to learn from their responses or even lack of responses and to make necessary adaptations. We revert to repeating directions over and over, or stating directions louder with the hope of making ourselves clear.

Because the spoken word exists for only an instant and is the symbolic, and abstract nature of language, the spoken word may elude many children with Down syndrome. In addition to having difficulty comprehending the word(s), the child may have a fluctuating or constant hearing loss, an auditory memory deficit, fewer memory channels, a need for increased processing time, and an inability to "filter out" irrelevant information. Therefore, the educator must utilize creative techniques to assist the student to compensate.[9]

Most children with Down syndrome are visual learners. As the saying goes, "A picture is worth a thousand words." Illustrations, symbols, pictures are effective tools for assisting a child to compensate for auditory memory deficits or fewer memory channels. Unlike the split second interaction with a spoken word, concrete visual cues may be used for as long as the child needs them.[9]

Caution! Frequently, visual learners are taught solely with visual techniques. However, should the student with Down syndrome receive only visual instruction, known auditory deficits will remain and may even increase. For example, if you were to be born with a weak right arm, would you continue to exercise only the strong arm? No, the goal would be to strengthen the weak right arm. Similarly, if a child is a strong visual learner, we must program specific instruction to build stronger auditory skills.[7]

The depth and breadth of characteristics that may influence responses of a child with Down syndrome are numerous. Therefore, the teacher must be a diagnostic clinician. Educators must train themselves to observe, evaluate, and synthesize all responses of the student with Down syndrome and to diagnose and prescribe the most appropriate and effective program of instruction.[12]

AUTHOR'S INSTRUCTIONAL SUGGESTIONS

1) Provide language labels for everything! Use word cards taped to objects, visual cues, illustrations, and pictures.

2) Read, read, read! Ask parents to commit to daily reading to their child.

3) Recognize that children with Down syndrome are passive learners. Anything you want to be learned must be taught.

4) Elicit parental participation in labeling the child's environment. This is an excellent ongoing homework assignment. Teach parents they can "never assume" unless they have taught the child a language label at a previous time.

5) Program instruction that incorporates distributed practice (ongoing review dispersed over time). Students with Down syndrome must experience ongoing review; otherwise, information will be dropped from long-term memory. Utilize distributed practice in all areas.

6) Evaluate channel capacity with both visual and auditory testing.

7) Utilize suggested channel capacity to determine the percent of new material that can be imposed on familiar

material to maintain the student's success level.

8) Give clear, concise directions slowly.

9) State the most important set of directions at the end of the direction sequence.

10) Provide students with adequate time to process information. WAIT.[9,12]

11) Evaluate all student responses carefully! include all the characteristics of an individual with Down syndrome in your list of diagnostic understanding prior to reacting.

12) Most students with Down syndrome are visual learners; develop instruction specifically to develop weaker auditory skills.

13) Improve sequencing skills through the use of pattern blocks, number patterns, pictures, games of concentration.

14) Identify memory skills as a goal. Use the established number of memory channels to design spelling lists. Letters per word and words per list will be determined by the number of channels a child can successfully manage.

15) Children with Down syndrome do not store and retrieve information easily. Frequently, I have observed a greater ability for children with Down syndrome to internalize whole units of information and then break those units apart, i.e., Michael learns a sight word (whole unit), then the beginning sound, and then the name for the beginning letter. This is the opposite of traditional sequence of teaching letter names, then letter sounds, and then building words.[9] Utilize new insights when designing the sequence of skill introduction. Traditional techniques may inhibit progress.

16) Train memory.[12] Ask questions that require memory practice, based on the number of memory channels.

- "After lunch, I will ask you to name two children you spoke to during recess."
- "Tomorrow, I will ask you to name three things you ate for dinner."
- "After the holidays, I want you to tell me about five presents you received."
- "After recess, I will ask you to tell me one game you played."

17) Remember that the receptive-expressive gap is inherent to many students with Down syndrome. Much like a stroke victim, there is a significant difference between receptive (comprehension) and expressive (verbalization) abilities. Envision an older person who has suffered a stroke. Tremendous frustration builds with the struggle to express themselves. This is how a child with Down syndrome may feel due to the receptive-expressive gap.

18) Read: Teaching Reading to Children with Down Syndrome.[9]

19) Read: Classroom Language Skills for Children with Down Syndrome.[4]

Concept Attainment[6]

Concepts organize diverse material into a meaningful order. When a person applies a concept, it demonstrates that he has attained understanding of the concept and bypassed the need to relearn the concept.

According to Jean Piaget, each child progresses through stages of development where various cognitive skills are acquired. Individuals with Down syndrome take longer to learn but show the same sequence of stages of concept attainment. Patterns develop at a slower rate. This necessitates attention to the

MENTAL AGE of Piaget's stages.[9]

Sensory motor (birth to 2 years) – The infant experiences the environment through sensory experiences and motor activities and learns to distinguish between him/herself and the world.

Preoperational (2 years to 6 years) – The child experiences the environment through the use of developing language skills. Memory skills are now in place, which helps to make sense of how the world is represented by language and symbols. The child remembers previous experiences and develops expectations.

Concrete Operations (7 years to 11 years) – Logic develops. The child learns to organize his/her thoughts by ordering and classifying. The child manipulates objects and needs hands-on activities to solve problems and learn cause-and-effect relationships.

Formal Operations (12 years plus) – The child uses abstract reasoning for the linking of concepts. The individual can mentally manipulate symbols rather than concrete manipulatives and can hypothesize and predict events and consequences.

Suggestions for Classroom Practice[6]

1) Children with Down syndrome learn best by actively participating, rather than sitting and listening.

2) Allow for manipulating of concrete materials to solve problems and maintain interest.

3) As learning occurs in an ordered sequence, tasks should be presented step by step, making sure that the child has the prerequisite concepts for the next step or level.

[6]Adapted from National Down Syndrome Society. The Educational Challenges Inclusion Study for the National Down Syndrome Society. New York: NDSS, 1996.

4) Be guided by the individual's mental age: his/her logic, interpretation of the problem, and expression of an answer may be different from what is expected at the individual's chronological age.

AUTHOR'S ADDITIONAL COMMENTS

Much like a staircase, the learning process is based on a foundation followed by a series of solidly built steps. First, there is sensory information, the *input* which corresponds to Piaget's Sensory Motor Stage – experiencing the environment through the senses. Then there is *perception*, the Preoperational Stage. The child experiences the environment through the process of organizing and interpreting sensory information and gives that information meaning. A language base develops and memory evolves. Subsequently, there is output, the *response*. The response requires the retrieval and use of stored information. As information is entered into our memory, it needs to be organized, related to other information, and then stored for future retrieval.

Robbie Blaha gave an example in a 1988 lecture that demonstrates the difficulties children with Down syndrome may have with these processes. She explained that we have mental files that enable us to store and retrieve information about any subject. She gave the example "Halloween." Just hearing the word Halloween stimulates us to retrieve our Halloween file. In that file are many subfiles that contain concepts such as decorations, colors, and parties.[9]

Ms. Blaha related that the children with whom she worked who were deaf and blind, many with mental retardation, did not have files. They had buckets. Her students stored Halloween memories without a category, without any organization, like grains of sand in a bucket, making retrieval difficult or impossible. This example clarifies some of the processing differences children with Down syndrome may have. For

[6]Adapted from National Down Syndrome Society. The Educational Challenges Inclusion Study for the National Down Syndrome Society. New York: NDSS, 1996.

example, if you ask a child with Down syndrome what she did on Halloween, she may not find the "concept" of Halloween in her mental files. She may have stored her Halloween experiences randomly, without organization, making retrieval difficult. She may remember specific information when prompted, "Did you go trick or treating? What costume did you wear?" Relationships between a costume, trick or treating, and Halloween may not have been made.[9]

Some children with Down syndrome do not recognize situational relationships and, therefore, do not have the concepts to understand the meaning of events. Additionally, language delays may limit vocabulary and the ability to assign file names to information for future use; students with Down syndrome may be unable to combine new information with other previously stored information in a category (file) for retrieval. Consequently, we must focus on helping the students organize information so they can effectively receive, file, store, and retrieve it.

Piaget's Concrete Operations Stage depicts the organizational processing required for classifying information and describes the emergence of logic. Piaget's developmental levels are sequential. The success in one stage is determined by the foundation of each prerequisite stage. A child must be able to experience his environment. He must be able to focus (attend) on sensory experiences. As those experiences acquire meaning through language labels, memory subsequently develops. As similar experiences are acquired, concepts develop. The child has then moved through the Sensory Motor, Preoperational and Concrete Operation stages. With mental and physical maturity, the child reaches Piaget's final stage, Formal Operations. Concepts are linked and abstract thinking occurs. This stage requires mental manipulation of symbols and will be the most difficult stage for children with Down syndrome. For this reason, the abstract nature of mathematics is often especially challenging for students with Down syndrome.

Individuals with Down syndrome take longer to learn but show the same sequence (Piaget's Developmental Stages) of concept attainment. However, their patterns develop at a slower rate, which necessitates attention to the mental age of Piaget's stages rather than the chronological age. For example, a 13 year old child with Down syndrome could be expected to need tokens, rods, or concrete items to solve math problems because he is still operating in the stage of concrete operations even though his chronological age would fall in the formal operation stage.[6]

Mental and chronological ages are found in student records; although we are taught not to look at student records, this information is a must for students with Down syndrome. The educator must have some idea of the student's mental age in each ability area in order to provide appropriate materials, instruction, and evaluation.

Teachers should <u>never</u> rely on a general ability label, i.e., mildly mentally handicapped, to reflect the child's ability in all subject areas! For example, psychological testing of a child with Down syndrome may indicate that communication skills (receptive, expressive, written) are in the mildly mentally handicapped range, daily living skills (personal, domestic) are in the mildly mentally handicapped range, socialization skills (interpersonal, play, coping) are in the low average range, mathematic reasoning is in the moderately mentally handicapped range, and basic reading (verbal reasoning) is in the mildly mentally handicapped range. A wide range of abilities exists in various areas of processing within the same child. Mildly mentally handicapped describes the general ability of the child. Abilities for all children vary. The abilities of a child with Down syndrome may vary to a greater degree than the typically performing student. Appropriate instructional design must be planned based upon suggested ability functioning. (Caution: psychological testing and student assessments may be skewed due to lack of sleep, illness, or other unknown factors.) Psychological testing indicators, in combination with classroom performance, will best determine the child's level of functioning. For example, psychological evaluations given after a holiday, a child's illness, or by an unknown tester may decrease the child's ability to perform. That child may be evaluated to be moderately mentally handicapped when, in fact, he is more accurately mildly challenged.

Never lower expectations based on psychological evaluations. Once, an Early Infant Stimulation teacher asked me what my goals for my son were. I replied that I wanted him to be provided with as many prereading experiences as possible, i.e., colors, textures, pictures, books. She responded, "Oh, don't get your hopes up too high." I was dumbfounded and replied, "If I don't keep my expectations high, who will?" My son has average, mild, and moderate ability ranges in various areas, and my son can read! It is the responsibility of the teachers, parents, and family to maintain high expectations within the limitations of the child's disability.

AUTHOR'S INSTRUCTIONAL SUGGESTIONS

1) Be guided by the child's suggested mental age.

2) **Allow adequate processing time. Wait.** Previously, I discussed the need to provide extra processing time. Think of your kitchen utensil drawer. Have you ever dug through all those gadgets totally confident that the gizmo you were looking for was hidden amongst the hundreds of gadgets entangled there? For children with Down syndrome who are not efficient in developing concepts and filing them for instant recall, this frustration must be a similar feeling. The child knows the information, but it may take some searching to locate it. Another analogy is one I call the teenager's "Oh Yeah" syndrome. When asking a question of most teenagers who are totally connected to the visual images on a computer screen, prior to a response, there is the head lifting to face you with a blank stare. After several seconds, you are given an answer, "Oh Yeah." Although the teenager heard the question, their attention was divided; therefore, the lapse of time for a response was longer.

3) Teach the child relationships using categorizing games, such as lotto, bingo, or jeopardy.

4) Partner with the speech therapist and parents. Identify the language labels for a category of words, such as kitchen, bedroom, or classroom. Have parents tape word card labels to items that relate to the category, i.e., kitchen: stove, refrigerator, sink, or cupboards or bedroom: bed, dresser, or desk.

5) Take field trips, field trips, field trips. Go to the music room, the cafeteria, gas station, farm, zoo, art museum, grocery store, fire station, and police station.

6) Make charts. Create word-webs.

7) Consider grade retention to allow primary students extra time to build solid language and memory foundations. Children with Down syndrome do mature much the same as typically performing students but at a slower rate. As the development of lasting peer relationships will be paramount during the middle and high school years, the most appropriate retention years are during the primary grade. Retention affords children extra time to establish sound academic foundations and allows them to continue to thrive throughout their school experience and graduate with an established peer group. Grade retention for all children is less traumatic during the primary school experience.

Mediational Strategies[6]

Every individual varies in his/her ability to organize thought processes, store information, and recall as needed. Children with Down syndrome have difficulty in these areas because it is heavily based on language and the ability to categorize. Presenting new material to be learned in groups or clustering material in an organized fashion helps to facilitate learning. Introducing a mediator which is a prompt or cue connecting the

stimulus or response to be learned helps to break down a
concept that is too abstract to grasp on its own.[6]

Suggestions for Classroom Practice[6]

1) Restructure or organize visual and/or auditory presentations
   to break down the relationships to basic concepts, such as
   size, shape, pattern, or categories.

2) Sequence activities from simple to complex with time lapses
   to facilitate responding from language or cognitive
   processing delays. Increasing response time allowed has
   been shown to improve learning abilities of slow learners
   (Judd and Bilsky, 1989).

3) Verbalize and repeat the instructional links between
   concepts.

4) Use meaningful, familiar, and relevant materials.

5) Repeat, rehearse, and drill often.

6) Employ and train mediational strategies.

Transfer of Learning[6]

Learning abilities of children with Down syndrome can be
improved through highly structured, meaningful activities that
are analyzed and sequenced from simple to complex.
Generalization of concepts to different situations is difficult.
Children with Down syndrome may have difficulty in recognizing
similarities between problems and situations. This deficit leads
to teachers reporting that their students learn something one
day but forget it the next. This behavior reflects lack of
transferring rather than learning.

---

[6]Adapted from National Down Syndrome Society. The Educational Challenges
Inclusion Study for the National Down Syndrome Society. New York: NDSS, 1996.

Suggestions for Classroom Practice[6]

1) Use meaningful materials and experiences to cut down on novelty which could confuse the learner.

2) Teach concepts in a variety of different learning environments and with different people, pointing out similarities and differences between them.

3) Use frequent review and repetition.

4) Practice newly learned skills with different people, materials, and environments.

5) Use both verbal explanations and performance activities.

AUTHOR'S ADDITIONAL COMMENTS

As stated above, "*Learning abilities of children with Down syndrome can be improved through highly structured, meaningful activities that are analyzed and sequenced from simple to complex.*"

This statement holds true for all learners. The imperative difference is that all the naturally acquired steps of a typically developing student must be taught to most students with Down syndrome. Crawling is a perfect example. We all know the saying, "You must crawl before you walk." Typically, the infant explores the environment by rolling, crawling, and then walking. For children with Down syndrome, these skills evolve through a tremendous amount of early intervention and practice. In other words, I helped my son learn to crawl. I moved one arm, one leg; then the other arm and the other leg. We crawled across the floor until I dripped with perspiration. We spent weeks practicing. The day Michael independently crawled across the floor was triumphant. Children with Down syndrome can and do learn and perform much the same as other children. The

[6]National Down Syndrome Society. The Educational Challenges Inclusion Study for the National Down Syndrome Society. New York: NDSS, 1996.

number of steps for skill acquisition may be greater and often requires the teaching of skills frequently taken for granted.

"Generalization of concepts to different situations is difficult. Children with Down syndrome may have difficulty in recognizing similarities between problems and situations."

I have received some interesting, upsetting, and frequently amusing calls and/or notes from school. One call began, "Mrs. Peoples, we are sorry to bother you, but we have a problem. Michael is teaching the children how to spit at recess." (Please know I am always grateful for the calls. Usually, the solutions are simple ones.) Upon arriving at school, I sat down to talk to Michael. I did not begin the conversation with a lecture on "spitting." I simply asked, "Why? Why were you spitting at recess, Michael?" In total innocence he replied, "Mom, remember Mike Fink does it in the movie, <u>Davy Crockett and the Riverboat Pirates</u>." (In the movie, Mike Fink has a spitting contest.) What appeared to be a problem was actually an inability to transfer appropriately what he saw and learned in the movie to a new setting. It took but one explanation to solve the spitting dilemma.

Recently, I had a perceptive discussion with Michael's teacher. His teacher indicated that the cafeteria monitors felt they had a problem, but she believed perhaps his behavior should be accepted as appropriate. Michael was the only one who packed lunch (due to Michael's increased tactile sensitivity, he eats a limited number of foods). He would enter the cafeteria, go to his table, and sit there. He would not eat until all the other children arrived with their trays. Explanations that he should begin eating when he arrived since he is a slower eater, or that he would be late for recess did not alter his behavior. His teacher smiled at me and asked, "Good manners?" I chuckled with delight. Michael has been taught at home to wait until everyone is served and seated before eating. Not only was his behavior acceptable; altering that behavior would create unneeded confusion for the manners I was teaching at home. Ultimately, Michael did not mind being late for recess.

A few years ago, I received a telephone call that was truly comical. Michael was working with his new, young, occupational therapist. While she was speaking to another teacher, she had given Michael a turkey baster filled with water and asked him to use it to make letters on the chalkboard. (Actually, this idea is great when carefully supervised.) Well, as you can imagine, Michael, armed with a baster, which to him was a squirt gun, created total havoc. With the teachers laughing and running from him, he thought they were playing. Two simple solutions were available. One, always supervise a child with water. Two, should the child misuse the water... remove it.

Understandably, in the situation above there was a lack of experience on the teacher's part, but plans must be well thought out and supervised. I think it is appropriate to interject at this time that not all my calls from school are amusing. I do not, and never will, have perfect children. However, Michael's behaviors require comprehensive analysis before response. Simply talking with Michael is not always the solution.

Unique overt behavior may not be the only evidence that the child with Down syndrome is unable to transfer and generalize information from one setting to another. Occasionally, teachers report that their students learned something one day but forgot it the next. This behavior may reflect lack of transferring rather than lack of learning. A student who has learned to count to ten using blocks may not transfer that ability to counting oranges in the grocery store without specific instruction. The ability to transfer learned knowledge from one situation to another will improve through the specific teaching of concepts in different learning environments and with different people, pointing out the similarities and differences between them.

Lack of transfer skills and concept attainment has also been documented with respect to reading instruction. Some children with Down syndrome who have learned letter sounds (printed letters eliciting an appropriate sound) do not comprehend how the letters go together to form a word. When asked to read a word, the student will make the sound of each letter but is unable to say the word. In other words, they are "stimulus bound," responding with only the isolated sounds they have been taught. The student cannot transfer their knowledge of letter sounds to actual words; thus, children do not understand the concept of reading. Patricia Oelwein writes in her book, <u>Teaching Reading to Children with Down Syndrome</u>, that in her limited experience with children who say letter sounds rather than words, she has not been successful in teaching them to read words. She, therefore, prefers to start with sight words.[9]

Armed with the knowledge that transfer of learning is difficult for children with Down syndrome, I strongly urge the acquisition of parental support for sharing their child's I.E.P. with <u>all</u> school personnel. The previously related personal examples demonstrate the need for cafeteria staff, recess monitors, nurses, and aides to have the necessary student information in order to respond appropriately and provide support for the IEP goals.

Inclusion experiences in science, for example, can be enhanced when the teacher is aware of IEP objectives. For example, a student objective may be to increase the pincher grasp (thumb and forefinger). This is not typically a goal of most science lessons. However, during a frog dissection in a third grade class, the child with Down syndrome may be expected to pick up and give dissection instruments or pins to students in his group. The student may also be asked to name (language labels) materials or parts of the frog. Goals of the IEP would be met, the student included, and appropriate subject adaptations implemented.

Extracurricular teachers (music, art, and gym), specialized subject teachers (math, science, and reading), and support staff cannot be expected to provide appropriate support for a student IEP if the information remains exclusively available to the case conference team. The case conference team of perhaps five persons reflects a small percentage of adult intervention experienced by an inclusion student in a day.

As IEP goals are established, include suggestions to aid the student in attaining "closure" in one subject/skill area prior to the introduction of another, i.e., changing from math to reading. Students with Down syndrome who become "stimulus bound" (focused on one skill) and who lack transfer skills may not naturally be prepared to begin a new subject without closure in the prior subject. Scheduled silent reading time between subjects has been successful in enabling the child with Down syndrome to refocus his attention providing closure in one area and allowing the teacher to subsequently redirect student attention to the next. Another successful technique is to engage the child in a tangible, physical activity, i.e., finger exercises, rhymes with finger movement, a few stretches. Because there are many areas to consider in IEP planning, however a well thought-out and complete plan will afford greater student success.[12]

When examining IEP goals, plan for the transition from grade to grade and/or from building to building. Transfer skill ability may also affect the student's ability to adjust to new teachers, new teacher expectations, and new settings. For instance, towards the end of a half-day kindergarten experience, the student's day may be extended by an hour to include staying for lunch and recess. Later the student's day may be lengthened to include lunch, recess, and one hour in the predetermined, first grade class for the following year. This allows the child to become familiar with the novel experiences of eating at school, having a recess, and adjusting to his next year's teacher.

Changing to a new school may require a similar plan. The IEP may be designed to allow the student with Down syndrome to initially visit the new school. Towards the end of the academic year prior to the move, provisions may be made to allow the student to tour the school, eat lunch at the new school, or attend an afternoon activity. Anticipating student needs will provide both an expedient and successful transition into a new classroom and/or school.

AUTHOR'S INSTRUCTIONAL SUGGESTIONS

1) Dissect lessons into their smallest component steps. Never take for granted that a step for skill acquisition has been naturally learned. <u>Teach all steps</u>.

2) Provide ongoing distributed practice to maintain skills level.

3) Carefully analyze all student behaviors prior to response.

4) Teach concepts in a variety of different environments and with a variety of different people.

5) Know that the IEP is the key to successful inclusion. All school personnel and parents should read/reread the child's IEP to learn how to include the student in every school activity and provide transfer and generalization of skills.

6) Provide transition opportunities for one subject prior to the introduction of another, i.e., silent reading, tangible and/or physical activities.

7) Plan for transitions and transferring of skills from subject to subject, classroom to classroom, grade level to grade level, and building to building.

Motivation[6]

Children with Down syndrome are sometimes characterized as "stubborn", "passive", or "disinterested". These labels can be misleading. Even before school begins, students with Down syndrome experience increased failure, due to challenging developmental milestones, such as crawling, walking, and talking. Typical behaviors traditionally associated with slow learners are that they learn to expect corrections/criticism; they react passively or impulsively by making stereotyped responses, such as selecting the first choice or saying, "I don't know;" they avoid situations prone for failure by asking to go to the bathroom, by cutting class, by saying they are tired; and they sometimes accept a lower level of success. Students experiencing constant correction and criticism may give up and wait for someone else to answer the problem or perform the task: "learned helplessness" is the result.

Suggestions for Classroom Practice[6]

1) Assign tasks that are appropriate to developmental level and are well explained.

2) Create a success-oriented atmosphere.

3) Use attractive, meaningful, familiar materials.

4) Allow students to participate in developing the rules or the design of the lessons.

5) Provide external cues and rewards, then gradually fade them, so the rewards become internally based, and the student remains motivated.

6) Discourage the students from constantly seeking help and reward independence.

7) Encourage social rewards by encouraging the development of friendships with peers.

8) Use positive language like "Try another way" or "Think it through again," rather than "You're wrong."

AUTHOR'S ADDITIONAL COMMENTS

"Operant learning" is learning that takes place as a result of the influence of the environment and can be measured by a change in behavior. We know learning has taken place when we observe a change in behavior and can measure this change. My son, Michael, previously could not crawl, but now he walks

[6]Adapted from National Down Syndrome Society. The Educational Challenges Inclusion Study for the National Down Syndrome Society. New York: NDSS, 1996.

across the room. He could not read, but now he can read 100 sight words. In these instances, operant learning took place. Michael learned these behaviors because of his experiences with the environment. His environment provides the opportunity and the motivation for him to learn new behaviors.[9]

Materials and instruction generally provide an opportunity for learning. Meaningful rewards (praise, hugs, clapping, food) provide the motivation that inspires the learner to want to do the activity. Reinforcement is a rewarding event that encourages a specific behavior and is contingent on the performance of this behavior.[9] For example, a child might earn computer time for coloring inside the lines of a picture. The reinforcement is the earned computer time.

It is important to understand that if a reward does not maintain or increase the targeted behavior, then it is not reinforcing (motivating). A reward that may be very reinforcing for the typically performing student may not be reinforcing for a child with Down syndrome. Some children may work hard for stickers. A student with Down syndrome may find stickers upsetting because of an inability to remove them from a sticker sheet or affix them to paper. Likewise, some children may be deterred from certain behavior by checks on the board, tickets, or threat of a lower grade. These consequences may have no meaning to a child with Down syndrome and, therefore, will not effectively alter behavior.

The principles of operant learning are very effective teaching techniques for children with Down syndrome. Students who receive consistent and controlled reinforcement dependent on the production of certain behaviors are more likely to learn those behaviors. If reinforcement is provided inconsistently, the behavior may be acquired more slowly, or an undesirable behavior may be learned instead.[9]

Since a child with Down syndrome may not have a cognitive concept to appreciate and understand the reward (grades) or consequence (checks on the board), he may have difficulty learning from contingencies. A child with Down syndrome may not be willing to work for traditional rewards because he does not find them interesting. The "reinforcer" that is used to encourage a specific behavior must actually be reinforcing.

Discussions with the parents of a child with Down syndrome may help to define effective reinforcers and consequences to promote student progress. Once identified, the rate of reinforcement, in the beginning, may need to be close to 100%, item-by-item. This rate should be employed at each new task level and reduced to line-by-line, and page-by-page. It is important that the teacher relax, have patience, and reward every single little success. Patience and positive reinforcement will prevent "quitting" behaviors.[12] Gradually, external cues and rewards can be reduced so the rewards become internally based, and the student remains motivated.

AUTHOR'S INSTRUCTIONAL SUGGESTIONS

1) Establish a response baseline; for example, Michael cannot read any sight words. You are then able to measure a change in behavior; for example, Michael can read ten sight words.

2) Utilize parental experience and suggestions to identify effective rewards and consequences.

3) Allow students to participate in developing rules or the design of the lesson.

4) Give **consistent** and **controlled** reinforcement.

5) Praise is absolutely the best motivator. Children with Down syndrome are also highly responsive to smiles, hugs, and clapping. One year during an IEP conference, a teacher suggested that one of Michael's objectives should be to stop hugging. (There is a difference between random, inappropriate hugging and a warm hug as a reward). I was not supportive of the idea. I had spent the better part of the

summer reading stories from <u>Chicken Soup for the Teenage Mind</u> to my family at dinner. The sole point of the book was to depict the value of hugging. After all, the best part of a bad day may be a warm and tender hug.

6) Be sure the student understands the contingency for a reward (orally read the story; *then* we will clap).

7) Use food as a reinforcement only with parental consent. Food is an effective reinforcer when the child does not understand the if/then concept, i.e., If you read the story, then you will have free time. The hard-to-motivate student may need a more immediate, tangible reinforcer in order to gain his attention to try to do the task so that he will realize he can indeed do it.[9]

   a) Parental consent must be obtained in order to identify possible food allergies and/or favorite foods that are indeed reinforcing. Once identified, use a small quantity for each desired response. Phase out the food as the student becomes self-motivated.

   b) Good judgment must be employed when using food as a contingency for a desired behavior as a means to overcome learned helplessness. Remember food is a reward, contingent upon the production of a desired behavior, as opposed to a "bribe" which is contingent upon an undesirable behavior.[9]

   c) Persons who are highly critical of food reinforcement may never have experienced educating the hard-to-motivate learner. Frequently, the hard-to-motivate child may be overweight and/or a behavior problem. In this situation, options must be weighed and balanced. Food reinforcement is merely an option to consider when presented with a highly challenging circumstance. It may work.[9]

8) Remain encouraging as skills are learned. The goal is to move the student closer to mastery while maintaining a successful environment. During skill acquisition, phrases, such as, "No, that's not right," "That's wrong," "Not that way," should never be used. Skill acquisition is a learning stage. If the child has not mastered the skill, then the number right or wrong is unimportant. Move the student closer to mastery by saying, "That's good, let's try it another way" or "Great effort, let's try again." Always, always remodel! Remember, teaching is sharing knowledge and promoting learning. Testing is evaluating and measuring what the student knows. **It is inappropriate to test during the teaching phase.**

Conclusion[6]

Learning is a process whereby practice or experience produces a change in behavior that is not due to maturation. It is a hypothetical construct that is difficult to measure except by observing performance. Individuals with Down syndrome usually perform below average on tests of intelligence and are also inefficient learners. They do not learn spontaneously from their experiences and need new concepts to be clearly presented in a sequenced format. They have slow processing of verbal information and limited retention of new concepts and details. Children with Down syndrome can benefit from education in regular classroom situations, however, and do make academic gains. Their learning problems are a result of differing learning styles rather than learning impediments. Use of teaching methods that involve physical participation and visual cues or objects is effective with learners with Down syndrome.

To summarize, the learning characteristics of children with Down syndrome are more similar to their regular education peers than they are different. However, language and motivational deficiencies may necessitate more highly structured, sequenced activities, with smaller bits of information presented at a time, and lots of reward and praise.

ADDITIONAL AUTHOR'S COMMENTS

For most children, learning occurs naturally as they interact with their environment and develop a sense of themselves and the world around them. Children internalize these experiences through the use of developing language skills. Language provides the avenue for a child to make sense of how the world and objects are represented by language and symbols. Logic develops. Thoughts are organized by ordering and classifying. The child physically manipulates objects to solve problems, thereby, learning cause and effect relationships. Mental maturation culminates in abstract reasoning and concept linking. The child can mentally manipulate symbols rather than concrete materials and can hypothesize, predict events and consequences.

NEVER ASSUME!

Children with Down syndrome are passive learners and may not acquire mental maturation without specific teaching. Read, remember, and design instruction to assist the child with Down syndrome to move through the sequence of learning steps.

Sequence of Learning Steps

STEP 1 – ATTENTION – Provide a learning foundation. Prepare instruction that develops prerequisite attention skills.

STEP 2 – MEMORY – Teach language labels required as the building blocks for memory skills.

STEP 3 – CONCEPT ATTAINMENT – Teach students how to relate and organize information (build concepts) so they can file, store, and retrieve information effectively.

[6]Adapted from National Down Syndrome Society. The Educational Challenges Inclusion Study for the National Down Syndrome Society. New York: NDSS, 1996.

STEP 4.- <u>TRANSFER OF LEARNING</u> – Teach concepts in a variety of different learning environments and with different people, all of whom must be familiar with the student's IEP.

STEP 5 – <u>MOTIVATION</u> – Identify **effective** reinforcers and consequences. At each new task level, employ 100% rate of reinforcement, i.e. item-by-item. Gradually reduce reinforcement so rewards become internally based.

Without your help, the child with Down syndrome may never reach his greatest potential. Your thoughtful instruction is imperative.

Recommendations for Practitioners[6]

Inclusion is a successful, acceptable option for most children with Down syndrome. Little difference, if any, is noticeable in a class between the children with Down syndrome and their typical peers as young children. They usually play and get along well with other children. Friendships are formed in the classroom situation and at recess.

In the lower and upper elementary grades, teacher concerns regarding inclusion can be separated into three areas: 1) providing intervention for speech and language difficulties; 2) gaining information from reading; and 3) improving math ability and problem solving skills.

Speech and Language[6]

Speech and language problems have been known to occur more frequently among individuals with Down syndrome. Most teachers report difficulties due to 1) articulation problems and 2) limited semantic concepts. Many children with Down syndrome have a protruding tongue, which affects the clarity of speech. Using contextual cues can help teachers to understand their students with Down syndrome, as well as asking the students to repeat what they say a little more slowly.

Children with Down syndrome also have frequent middle ear infections, which can cause conductive hearing losses that can result in delayed language and speech problems. Semantic concepts can also be delayed due to their focusing on auditory language sequences (actual words and sounds), rather than underlying semantic or conceptual aspects (meaning). This delay can eventually lead to frustration with language and disruptive behavior.

The implications for teachers is that care must be given to the way directions for activities are explained, or questions are asked (e.g., circle the, in front of the...), as students with Down syndrome may have delayed language concepts. Also, if a student is being disruptive, it could be because they are not processing the language of the lesson. Sometimes, using a visual aid can help to convey the concept.

Reading[6]

Reading is made up of several components which may be more difficult for students with Down syndrome: 1) sensory/ perceptual (hearing the sounds, seeing the letters); 2) sequential (left to right, top to bottom on page and also grammar rules for meaning); 3) experiential (vocabulary, understanding of concepts); 4) learning/association (linking what is read to real life situations, transferring and generalizing information); and 5) affective (reading for pleasure, attitudes and interests). Students with Down syndrome may need help focusing their attention on reading activities and sustaining their attention over a period of time. When teachers break the story down into smaller parts and give a purpose for reading each part, it helps to motivate the student. Individual pacing helps a student feel more accepted as part of the group. Also, frequent review and rereading help facilitate comprehension.

[6]Adapted from National Down Syndrome Society. The Educational Challenges Inclusion Study for the National Down Syndrome Society. New York: NDSS, 1996.

Suggestions for Classroom Practice[6]

1) Use previous experiences of students to select reading topics.

2) Teach vocabulary words in context and review frequently.

3) Provide a variety of experiences to encourage rereading for practice, such as paired reading or role playing.

4) Encourage students to self-monitor their own reading and ask questions.

5) Ask students to sequence the events of the story.

6) Teach students to use contextual cues for comprehension.

7) Encourage writing and retelling of the stories.

8) Have students predict expectations for what they read.

9) Use multiple-choice questions to assess reading comprehension if writing is difficult for the child.

Math Skills[6]

In order to better understand how children with Down syndrome learn math skills, it is helpful to separate them into two areas: 1) arithmetic/computational skills and 2) word problem solving/concepts.

Arithmetic computation involves two distinct processes that entail different skills. When a student first learns how to perform an arithmetic skill, he/she learns the procedures for performing the operation or computation. Once these skills are repeatedly practiced, the computation is stored in a memory network and becomes part of that student's "declarative knowledge." The student with Down syndrome has great

[6]Adapted from National Down Syndrome Society. The Educational Challenges Inclusion Study for the National Down Syndrome Society. New York: NDSS, 1996.

difficulty achieving the stage of declarative knowledge and will often learn something only to forget it the next day. Sometimes a visual cue or "song" helps to prompt the computational memory. It is also helpful to allow the student with Down syndrome to use as many manipulatives or concrete activities as possible to physically perform or experience the computation. Peer tutoring and computer assisted instruction can also motivate the student.

The solution of arithmetic word problems is an area of difficulty for many students with Down syndrome. Solving word problems is made up of two abilities: 1) understanding what is being asked and 2) selecting and implementing a solution strategy. The first ability is heavily dependent on language and math concepts linked to vocabulary. In order to help a student with Down syndrome, teachers should explain the language or the vocabulary of the problem first. Again, a visual aid or concrete manipulative may be helpful to give an example. Memory is also a factor in this ability, so it may be helpful to repeat the problem or allow enough time for language processing. The second ability relates to recognizing the type of problem being asked (addition, subtraction, multiplication, division), pulling out the relevant factors of the problem, and performing the correct operation for solution. Rehearsal and repetition of practical problems can be helpful to prepare the student for future real-life math skills. Since transfer and generalization of a skill is also an issue, care should be taken to role play or to visit the exact environment in which the skill will have to be performed (e.g. restaurant, store).

Suggestions for Classroom Practice[6]

1) Look at individual common error patterns to try to decipher concept deficiencies.

2) Practice skills continually for fluency and repetition.

[6]Adapted from National Down Syndrome Society. The Educational Challenges Inclusion Study for the National Down Syndrome Society. New York: NDSS, 1996.

3) Make sure the student has the developmental prerequisites, such as one-on-one correspondence, more or less, quantity and numeration precedes computation skill.

4) Encourage the students to learn different problem solving strategies, pointing out commonalities and differences in concepts.

5) Show and label common word problem-solving formats that can cue certain operations, such as addition and subtraction (e.g., "all together," "fewer than").

6) Teach the child how to identify relevant and ignore extraneous information in math problems.

AUTHOR'S ADDITIONAL COMMENTS

Reading is made up of several performance skills that are all prerequisite to the presentation of academic materials. These performance skills develop naturally in most typical learners. We can never assume that a child with special needs will passively develop performance skills without specific training.[12]

AUTHOR'S INSTRUCTIONAL SUGGESTIONS

1) Evaluate ability in each performance area. Design specific training exercises to improve deficiencies prior to academic instruction.
2) Evaluate channel capacity with both visual and auditory testing.

3) Coordinate speech pathology programs with reading vocabulary development through a cooperative teaching approach.

[6]Adapted from National Down Syndrome Society. The Educational Challenges Inclusion Study for the National Down Syndrome Society. New York: NDSS, 1996.

4) Provide sound reinforcement of vocabulary development through routinely scheduled leisure reading times.

5) Provide for generalization of reading topics through experiences that allow students with reading challenges to practice transfer and generalization of learning.

6) Initially increase comprehension skills through the use of closed answered questions (yes/no). The difficulty of comprehension questions should move from simple to more complex over a period of time. Answering open-ended questions is ultimately the goal. Responses should be accepted in verbal, written, or artistic form depending on the child's skills.

7) Ask students to sequence the events of a story. Sequencing experiences should start with one or two items (pictures) and be expanded to more complicated sequencing over time. Sequencing skills are important to the development of memory and organizational skills and should be routinely included in lesson designs.

8) Students with Down syndrome create interesting journal entries. Any response generated should be accepted as good. Initially students may use unrecognizable symbols to write stories. The teacher should ask the student to read what he/she has written and simultaneously write down what is read. The student and teacher copies should be stored together for future rereading. All copies should be saved to create the student's journal.

9) At every level, a comprehensive reading program that has been designed with long-term scope and sequence must be implemented. It is far better to have a program that fails than no program at all. An eclectic approach to reading is simply unacceptable. Little progress is made and developing skills may diminish.

10) Refer to materials (i.e., games, exercises) specifically
designed and appropriate for children with Down syndrome.
See Oelwein[9], Kumin[4], and Wehrli[12].

Concluding Remarks

Recent trends in education and attitudes have become more
accepting of differently-abled students. This study has shown
that the inclusion of students with Down syndrome in typical
education classes is a valid option for educational programming.
However, much administrative support is needed to provide
well-planned transitions and training of personnel. Good
communication among parents and the multitude of
professionals is the key to success with inclusion.

The learning characteristics of students with Down syndrome
are more similar to their regular education peers than they are
different. However, language and motivational deficiencies may
necessitate more highly structured, sequenced activities with
smaller bits of information presented at a time and lots of
rewards and praise built into the design of the lesson.
Meaningful, familiar materials work best when adequate time is
allowed for processing a response.

Almost all of the teachers reported that they enjoyed the
experience of teaching the student with Down syndrome.
Teachers found the students responsive and eager when given
any kind of encouragement. There were reported differences in
learning styles that necessitated some modifications such as
fewer questions, different expectations, and simplified
curriculum. One teacher stated, "The best advice I could give to
any new inclusion teacher would be to keep calm, gather all of
the information you can about the student, and be enthusiastic
and flexible." Another teacher summed up her response by
saying, "I found inclusion to be the single most interesting and
rewarding experience of my teaching career. I would advise new
inclusion teachers to make friends with the students and go
with the flow." The general consensus among educators is that
"inclusion is a lot of work, but definitely worth it."

Final Author's Comments

It is imperative to every student that a sound foundation of performance skills be developed prior to and during the presentation of academic materials. Lessons must be designed and implemented to target deficiencies in

- Visual skills
  - Tracking– The ability to visually follow a left-to-right linear field. (Right to left progression.)
  - Discrimination – The ability to identify a specific symbol or set of symbols from a group with similar features, i.e. n, n, m, n.
- Language development – The progression of verbal output skills, i.e., vocabulary usage: number of syllables in a word, number of words used in a sentence.
- Auditory discrimination – The ability to filter out external environmental noises from a targeted auditory cue with comprehension, i.e., listening to and following oral directions.
- Pacing – Teacher-established rate at which students work.
- Ability to follow directions – Heavily based on auditory skills.
- Memory – The ability to store and retrieve (upon demand) previously experienced sensations and perceptions.

With a solid foundation of performance skills, the student is prepared to climb the steps of the learning staircase. The climb is not an easy one for children with Down syndrome. However, children with Down syndrome can and do succeed with the skillful encouragement of dedicated teachers.

Teachers do make a difference! Once, I was stopped in a grocery store by an acquaintance. Looking at Michael, she said, "Oh, I'm so sorry." I looked at her and replied, "My goodness no, you don't know what you're missing." I offer these thoughts to all teachers:

Truly, until you've enjoyed teaching a student with Down syndrome, you don't know what you're missing!

Bibliography

1. "The A to ZZZ of Attention Disorder." Reader's Digest. June, 2002 p. 44.

2. Cohen, William I., ed. Health Care Guidelines for Individuals with Down Syndrome: 1999 Revision. New York: National Down Syndrome Society, 1999.

3. Ginott, Haim G. Teacher and Child. New York: Collier, 1995.

4. Kumin, Libby. Classroom Language Skills for Children with Down Syndrome. Bethesda: Woodbine, 2001.

5. National Down Syndrome Society. Down Syndrome Facts and Resources. New York: NDSS.

6. National Down Syndrome Society. The Educational Challenges Inclusion Study for the National Down Syndrome Society. New York: NDSS, 1996.

7. National Down Syndrome Society. Friendship Knows No Boundaries. New York: NDSS.

8. National Down Syndrome Society. Speech and Language in Infants, Toddlers and Young Children with Down Syndrome. New York: NDSS, 2002.

9. Oelwein, Patricia. Teaching Reading to Children with Down Syndrome. Bethesda: Woodbine, 1995.

10. UPS for DownS. How Do I Talk about Down Syndrome? Des Plaines: UPS for DownS, 1996.

11. Wolff, LuVerne, et al. Fundamentals of Nursing. 7th ed. Philadelphia: Lippincott, 1983.

12. Wehrli, Kitty. Clinical Observation, Wehrli Institute. Fort Wayne. 1999-2003.

All St★rs Of Success Programs have been **specifically designed** to meet the learning needs of children with Down syndrome and other developmental delays.

Learning progress increases when opportunities for failure are reduced.

HOME
BEGINNING SIGHT WORD READING SERIES
CLASSROOM

Sight words are frequently used words that cannot be learned through the use of a picture. Approximately 220 basic sight words make up 50 to 75 percent of the words in material used by elementary school students. These words must be recognized at a glance, without stopping to sound them out before a child can read with confidence.

Readers that learn the most commonly used sight words will have mastered 50-75% of <u>all</u> words encountered in elementary reading material. The Stars Of Success Beginning Sight Word Reading Program has been meticulously designed for developmentally delayed children whose reading success may be at a sight word level for a greater length of time than the typically performing student.

All children are required to learn sight words. However, the Stars Of Success Beginning Sight Word Reading Program allows children experiencing educational challenges to be <u>included</u> in a true reading experience, similar to their peers, until they are developmentally ready to learn the more difficult elements of reading and phonics.

EVERYONE R.E.A.D.S.
The Stars Of Success Program difference:

Review: Each introduced sight word is practiced **six** times in every introductory book. The Series provides an individualized reading program format by offering a Book A-*first review book* and/or a Book B-*second review book* for each set of introduced sight words.

Exclusively sight word based: Beginning reader text has been created **exclusively** from previously introduced sight words.

Assessment: Evaluation forms for **sight word mastery** and **cumulative sight word mastery** are provided.

Distributed practice: Planned **ongoing practice** over time is an imperative component for children with short and long term memory deficits. All mastered words are pulled forward into future readers and subsequent reading series.

Success: Opportunities for failure are reduced when reading text is generated from previously mastered sight words.

St★rs Of Success reading series, sight word lists, and evaluations are available for review on our website: www.specialoffspring.com.

St★rs Of Success

HOME

SPELLING PROGRAM

CLASSROOM

Developmentally delayed children often are assigned spelling words they cannot read. Reading the word is a **<u>prerequisite skill</u>** to spelling the word. All Stars Of Success words are sight words previously mastered in the prerequisite Stars of Success Beginning Sight Word Reading Series. Not only can students successfully recognize and read each spelling list word prior to spelling demands, but they can also read every word in the student spelling books.

EVERYONE S.P.E.L.L.S.

The Stars Of Success Program difference:

Spelling words: Each spelling word list corresponds to the sequence of sight words in Beginning Sight Word Readers. As both programs are based on the same sight word list, children are able to experience reading and spelling successes much sooner than those provided by traditional programs.

Practice: Four practice activity pages are provided for each unit: Spell, Check, and Correct; Visual Memory/Visual Discrimination; Word Meaning; and Spelling Practice.

Evaluation: Assessment forms for **weekly** and **cumulative** list word mastery are included.

Limited spelling word lists: The number of spelling words presented in each lesson corresponds to the number of pieces of information research has demonstrated to be successful for many developmentally delayed children.

Lesson Design: Specific visual memory and discrimination lessons are included in each lesson to increase memory and attention skills.

Success: Distributed practice is incorporated into each spelling lesson to assure the maintenance of mastered spelling skills.

St★rs Of Success Student Spelling Books, corresponding reading series, and mastered sight words lists are available for review on our website: www.specialoffspring.com.

St★rs Of Success

HOME

HANDWRITING PROGRAM

CLASSROOM

In contrast to many commercial handwriting programs, only the Stars Of Success Handwriting Program has been designed to address the specific physical needs of developmentally delayed children resulting from low muscle tone, muscle hypotonia. Preschool and kindergarten students traditionally begin writing by recreating letters of the alphabet. With practice most students will easily achieve the expected mastery. Left untreated, however, the muscle hypotonia experienced by developmentally delayed children will continue to impede writing progress.

EVERYONE W.R.I.T.E.S.

The Stars Of Success Program difference:

W*riting components:* — Meticulously designed 15 minute, distraction-free lessons and muscle training activities bridge the gap between traditional handwriting programs and the physical needs of developmentally delayed children.

R*efine muscle skills:* — Instruction of children with Down syndrome and other developmental delays is based on the premise: Everything you want to be learned must be taught. Each writing skill is broken into its smallest component pieces to assure student success.

I*solation of target muscles:* — Daily physical therapy activities teach the student how to isolate and control the small muscles in the wrist and fingers.

T*herapy:* — Muscle therapy is incorporated into each practice session to refine isolated muscle control as student handwriting demands increase.

E*valuation:* — A comparison of daily, weekly, and monthly student handwriting and coloring performance will reveal student progress.

S*equential steps:* — All writing skills are presented from simple to complex to promote student success.

St★rs Of Success Handwriting Books

Lines Only - Book 1: Prewriting

Building With Lines - Book 2: Capital Letters

Lines on Lines - Book 3: Lowercase Letters

are available for review on our website: www.specialoffspring.com.

4 HOUR SEMINARS

Success is the key!

OVERVIEW

- Overview of six learning processes (NDSS Educational Challenges Study)
    - Attention
    - Memory
    - Concept attainment
    - Mediational strategies
    - Transfer of learning
    - Motivation
- Formatting instruction effectively to accommodate know deficiencies.
    - Distributed practice
    - Pacing
    - Increased processing time.
- Relating developmental stages to the scope and sequence of instructional design.
- Evaluating and planning for the mastery and maintenance of skills.
- Relating student behavior directly to lesson design.

FULL DAY WORKSHOP
"CEU" ELIGIBLE

EDUCATORS: all persons who interact with children who have developmental delays.

Designing Instruction to Meet the Specific Learning Needs Characteristic of Children with Down Syndrome And Other Developmental Delays
Susan J. Peoples

OVERVIEW

- Session 1
    - Identification of specific learning needs characteristic of children with Down syndrome and other developmental delays and their academic impact.
    - Designing instruction to target specific learning needs.
- Session 2
    - Overview of six learning processes (NDSS Educational Challenges Inclusion study)
    - Formatting instruction to effectively accommodate known deficiencies
- Session 3
    - Relating developmental stages to the scope and sequence of instructional design.
    - Capitalizing on student strengths and successes in the design of initial reading programs.
    - Planning for reading inclusion during periods of prolonged maturation.
- Session 4
    - Programming for individual student needs: handwriting, reading, spelling.
    - Evaluating and planning for the mastery and maintenance of skills.
    - Designing, formatting, and implementing spelling programs.

E-mail: specialoffspring@aol.com for details.

About the Speaker
Susan J. Peoples

As an educator for 30 years (B.S. in elementary education and post-graduate studies), research clinician, author, and parent of a child with Down syndrome, Ms. Peoples has spent ten years exploring, evaluating, and designing curricular materials and methods to improve the educational experience of children with Down syndrome and other developmental delays.

Ms. Peoples has been a featured speaker at numerous schools and conferences, including the National Down Syndrome Society (NDSS) 2003 Annual Conference, the 2004 Annual Greater St. Louis Down Syndrome Association Conference, the Phoenix 2005 Down Syndrome Network Conference, the Kansas City Down Syndrome Guild 2005 Conference, the 2005 NDSS Nebraska Conference, the Chicago UPS for Downs 2006 Conference, and the Cleveland Upside of Downs 2006 Conference.

... *"Not only did my husband and I attend but also some of the para's at our son's school attended. What a huge turn around we have seen since the seminar. Our son's behavior has turned around, and he is now reading sight words! We are thrilled with his new progress."*

> Thanks,
> The Studley Family
> Ottawa, KS

VALUABLE RESOURCES NOT LISTED IN BIBLIOGRAPHY OF <u>STARS OF SUCCESS</u>

Little Giant Steps (Excellent auditory and visual memory programs.)

info@littlegiantsteps.com
(972) 758-1260

Talk Tools (An outstanding oral motor program targeting speech and feeding needs.)

www.talktools.net
(888) 529-2879

Lose The Training Wheels (Superior program providing <u>all</u> the steps required for bicycling success.)

www.losethetrainingwheels.org

Woodbine House Publishers (Publishing house for children who have disabilities.)

www.woodbinehouse.com
(800) 843-7323

"Every era is guided by a mode of thought. This Millennium, I Just Am defines the movement for a more humane society. Deserving of great literary awards, this text must be included in every school and public library!"

Susan J. Peoples

I Just Am
A STORY OF DOWN SYNDROME AWARENESS AND TOLERANCE

Bryan and Tom Lambke

with a forward by
Shannon D. R. Ringenbach, Ph.D.
Department of Kinesiology Arizona State University

and introduction by
Cheryl Rogers-Barnett,
daughter of
Roy Rogers and Dale Evans

For ordering information:
Five Star Publications, Inc.
P.O. Box 6698
Chandler, AZ 85246-6698

Phone: 480-940-8182
Toll Free: 866-471-0777

On the Web:
www.FiveStarPublications.com
www.IJustAm.org